America
the
Vulnerable

America
the
Vulnerable

The Threat of Chemical and Biological Warfare

Joseph D. Douglass, Jr.

AND

Neil C. Livingstone

Lexington Books

D.C. Heath and Company/Lexington, Massachusetts/Toronto

Library of Congress Cataloging in Publication Data

Douglass, Joseph D.
America the vulnerable.

Bibliography: p.
Includes index.
1. Chemical warfare.   2. Biological warfare.
3. United States—Defenses.   4. Terrorism.   I. Livingstone, Neil. C.   II. Title.
UG447.D68   1987   358'.34   85-45615
ISBN 0-669-12080-4 (alk. paper)

Published simultaneously in Canada
Printed in the United States of America
Casebound International Standard Book Number: 0-669-12080-4
Library of Congress Catalog Card Number: 85-45615

The paper used in this publication meets the minimum requirements of
American National Standard for Information Sciences—Permanance
of Paper for Printed Library Materials, ANSI Z39.48-1984. ∞™

ISBN 0-669-12080-4

87 88 89 90 91 8 7 6 5 4 3 2 1

Contents

Foreword

Robert L. Pfaltzgraff, Jr.
President,
Institute for Foreign Policy Analysis, Inc.

T he present international security environment is characterized by the convergence of a series of phenomena, the net effect of which is to produce a new threat to the United States and other nations. The late twentieth century is an era in which advanced technology provides the means to produce weapons of unprecedented lethality available to state and nonstate actors nearly on a global scale. In turn, the growth of such weaponry occurs in a security context in which there are numerous existing and potentially explosive conflicts, the sources of which are often complex and the outcome of which is of direct importance to the United States. Indeed, the United States, including not only its governmental officials but also its civilians, has become the object of various forms of low-intensity warfare.

The use of chemical and biological weapons, or the threat to do so, is deeply rooted in the history of warfare. Earlier in the twentieth century, in particular between the two World Wars, there was an almost obsessive preoccupation with such capabilities that grew out of the experience on the battlefields of the Western Front in World War I, resulting in casualties by the thousands and the meticulously recorded descriptions of the effects of the use of such agents in warfare as well as the accounts of those who had been the object of such attack.

The horror with which peoples around the world, and nowhere more than the United States, have viewed chemical and biological weapons accords with our quest for a world safe from apocalyptic death and disabling disease—the antithesis of the effects of such weapons if they are actually employed in battle rather than, as in the case of the Western allies in the Second World War, constituting the basis for deterring their use by others. By their very nature, chemical and biological weapons offend a society whose ethics include a deeply held conviction that the physical sciences, and medicine in particular, must be used for the eradication of disease and the advance of health and life expectancy. Nevertheless, there has been mounting evidence of the employment of such capabilities in recent years—for example in the Iran-Iraq war and by the Soviet Union against hapless peoples in Afghanistan and in Southeast Asia. Modern science has conferred unprecedented means for the use of weapons not to contain pestilence, but to spread it—not to eliminate existing disease but to create ever new agents having temporary or permanent incapacitating effects on human beings.

The chemical and biological capabilities wrought by advanced technology constitute a threat whose full dimensions have yet to become apparent either within or outside the official policy community in the United States. In the hands of terrorist groups, such means have already begun to constitute what the authors of this volume have termed "the poor man's atomic bomb." Building upon a shorter monograph published in 1984 by the Institute for Foreign Policy Analysis, Joseph D. Douglass, Jr., and Neil C. Livingstone have produced a work that, precisely because it is frightening in the potential implications of technologically advanced chemical and biological weapons, deserves to be widely read not only for its insights but also for the policy options provided by the authors. Combining a detailed knowledge of some of the latest trends in chemical and biological weapons with hypothetical situations or scenarios, they set forth a series of possible uses, together with the likely consequences that would follow, for the United States and other countries. The analysis is developed within a global strategic framework in which U.S. interests are the object of attack abroad and at home. The value of the volume is enhanced by the broadening of the discussion of chemical and biological weapons to encompass the prevailing drug culture—which itself constitutes a clear and present danger to the socio-political fabric of the United States. According to the authors, the increasing sophistication of drugs, included so-called "designer drugs," must be seen as part of a broader effort by America's enemies to erode from within the political and social will of the nation. There exists what has been termed a Nark-Intern (Narcotics International)—a series of international networks by which drugs are transported for sale in the United States and else-where—in which the Soviet Union and its client states have played a role of central and, according to the authors, decisive importance.

The contents of this volume do not make happy reading. It is not essential to agree in full with their policy options to recognize the importance nevertheless of addressing in comprehensive fashion the formidable security problems examined. The conclusions and policy recommendations in themselves are controversial. Together the analysis and options set forth by Joseph Douglass and Neil Livingstone furnish the basis for the examination of an issue of increasing importance for the United States in the late twentieth century. The authors have provided a vitally important contribution to the national security community by integrating the issues of chemical and biological weapons, the drug culture, and international terrorism within a strategic perspective. Thus they have furnished the *sine qua non* for a necessary formulation of an American strategy without which the fictional vignettes so skillfully employed as heuristic devices in this volume could become the reality of the international and domestic landscape of the future.

Preface

Horresco referens ("I shudder at the very thought of it").

—Virgil, *Aenid*, book II

The ambassador to an Arab nation from a Far Eastern country was approached at a reception in Bonn, West Germany, by one of the other guests, and the two men struck up a conversation. The guest asked the ambassador if he knew a mutual "friend," a top Arab official. Receiving an affirmative response, the guest wanted to know whether the ambassador would be kind enough to carry back a highly valuable gift to the Arab official: a rare copy of the Koran. The ambassador agreed to do so, and delivered the Koran to the Arab official upon returning to the country to which he was accredited.

The Arab official, however, was a careful man, and he sent the Koran to be checked out by his security detail. They found, much to their shock and surprise, that the pages of the holy book had been treated with a deadly poison. Had the Arab official thumbed through the book and touched his fingers to his lips as he turned the pages, he would almost certainly have died.

How much of the above story is true is difficult to ascertain. The sources are reliable. However, much of what happens in the eerie world of chemical, biological, and toxin warfare and related intelligence operations is not public information. In many cases such information has been deliberately suppressed by frightened governments. Other times, it is simply not recognized for what it really is. What is important is that the above story is entirely possible given existing technology.

We live in a world where it is possible to assassinate someone with a microscopic pellet containing a poison thousands of times more deadly than nerve gas, or with a greeting card containing micro-capsules inside that snap when the card is opened, releasing a lethal chemical agent. It is even possible to kill someone by saturating their clothing with a virulent poison while at the dry cleaners; the poison is later absorbed through the victim's skin.

Though not a terrorist incident, the tragedy at Bhopal is clear evidence of the mayhem that could be created by deliberately sabotaging a modern chemical production facility, or by using industrial chemicals as battlefield weapons. As product tampering becomes more and more commonplace, we have to anticipate the day when terrorists or other malefactors, using recently developed techniques, lace common food or pharmaceutical products with viruses causing AIDS or other dread diseases. Indeed, prosecutors in Florida recently charged two men with conspiracy to commit murder after they allegedly poured AIDS-infected blood serum into another man's coffee.

We are entering an era when even the smallest nation or terrorist group may be armed with chemical or biological (or biochem) weapons of mass destruction, in some cases giving them military parity with the major powers. There is an arms race going on in the Third World today of unprecedented proportions, as nations such as North Korea, Iran, Ethiopia, Syria, and even Peru seek "ultimate" weapons. North Korea, for example, has five plants producing both lethal and incapacitating chemical agents. Even more frightening, the Soviet Union is engaged in a massive effort to develop "Andromeda"-like viruses and toxins by utilizing genetic engineering techniques. These agents are capable of ravaging the globe, and whosoever holds the antidotes will prevail.

According to a report submitted by the Defense Department to the House Permanent Select Committee on Intelligence in August 1986, the Soviet Union is engaged in routine and systematic violation of the 1972 international convention banning biological and toxin weapons. Such agents, tailored to military specifications, can be manufactured cheaply and rapidly in small laboratories with self-cleaning equipment, maintains the report, making it impossible "for anyone to prove that a given substance has been produced."

Not only is the USSR stockpiling frightening new offensive agents for possible use against the West, but the Soviets and their surrogates are employing a variety of chemical and toxin agents in the Third World. For more than a decade, reports emanating from Kampuchea, Laos, and Afghanistan have described aircraft that shower insurgents and villagers with red, orange, or yellow dust, thought to be a mycotoxin that produces sickness and even death.

This book will examine the scientific developments that have so radically altered the strategic balance, and detail Soviet intentions with respect to the use of chemical, biological, and toxin weapons. Moreover, the threat to U.S. security posed by terrorists armed with chemical and biological (C/B) weapons, and the murky world of secret intelligence operations where such weapons have been employed, will be described. The rapidly escalating C/B arms race in the Third World will also be explored. Finally, in viewing drug and narcotics trafficking as a form of chemical warfare, careful scrutiny will be given to communist involvement in the production, refinement, and distribution of dangerous drugs to the West.

While the United States debates the development of a massive defensive effort against nuclear attack (the Strategic Defense Initiative), the fact remains that this nation is almost entirely defenseless against chemical, biological, and toxin weapons of mass destruction. Some of these weapons may already be secreted within our borders; others could be synthesized by our enemies within a matter of hours, or days at the most. Indeed, it is doubtful that most biological attacks would even be recognized for what they are. Even if it could be proven with certainty that the outbreak of a particular disease was not a natural occurrence and instead was deliberately instigated, it would be almost impossible to pinpoint the exact source.

The material contained in this book is not footnoted, so as not to leave a roadmap for would-be terrorists. In other cases, information has been provided by government sources with the understanding that there be no direct attribution, either for political reasons or to avoid compromising sensitive human sources. The manuscript was discussed with numerous experts, both in and out of government. Most sources and experts who provided assistance also expressed their desires to remain anonymous. The subject is simply too sensitive; its implications, too mind-boggling. The United States is just beginning to acknowledge the scope and seriousness of the problem. Most other nations are reluctant to even address the subject at all, or to inquire into Soviet violations of international agreements.

Once the problem is recognized, then there is the challenge of what to do about it. For many policymakers, there are few, if any, constructive measures that can be taken to lessen U.S. vulnerability to C/B weapons, and even those measures are regarded as so unpalatable as to be out of the question. Contrary to such negative thinking, we have offered a modest agenda for addressing the chemical-biological-toxin threat. We emphasize that this agenda represents only a first step, but as with all journeys, it is often the first step that is the most difficult.

There is no safety in delay—only ruin. What is important is that action no longer be deferred, and that the problem be addressed forthrightly and without illusion. The evidence is overwhelming as to America's present vulnerability.

Acknowledgments

I n January 1984 the Institute for Foreign Policy Analysis, Inc., published our study *CBW: The Poor Man's Atomic Bomb*. The response to this study was unusually strong and surprisingly positive. As several policy specialists within the government remarked, it was time for someone to bring the issue of CBW terrorism out of the closet and alert the government and public to the potential dangers. We would like to extend our thanks and appreciation to Dr. Robert L. Pfaltzgraff, Jr., president of the Institute of Foreign Policy Analysis for his support in publishing that study and then encouraging us to expand the monograph into a book that would examine, in an equally forthright manner, the full range of chemical and biological warfare issues that have emerged in the past decade, but which, for the most part, have been deliberately kept out of the public spotlight. Most of the original study is incorporated into the section on terrorism that appears at the beginning of the book.

We also thank our many colleagues and friends in government, the media, academia, and private industry who have also encouraged us to tell this story and have provided many suggestions and critical insights. Especially, we want to thank Jan Sejna for sharing with us his invaluable insight into Soviet strategy and decision making. Harvey J. McGeorge is also due special thanks for providing numerous illustrations and important real-life examples. We hope the reader will find the final product provocative and, to a certain degree, alarming, because that is the essence of the subject. We believe alarm is entirely appropriate and essential if the topics are to receive the serious attention they deserve before a real crisis, which the nation is presently ill prepared to manage, arises.

Introduction
The Lure of Chemical
and Biological Warfare

Chemical and biological agents are simultaneously the most sinister yet beckoning agents of human destruction. They are sinister because they are so quietly effective—ultimate weapons designed to attack the very essence of life. They are beckoning for exactly the same reason, and because they are cheap and can be employed in many different ways (including covertly).

Mention chemical warfare, and the image that springs to mind is World War I when the Germans initiated the first mass use of chemical agents in battle in the vicinity of Ypres. The use escalated and by the end of the war, 1.3 million men had been wounded by gas, and ninety-one thousand had died. Had the Germans only known how to exploit the use of gas, the outcome of the war might have been quite different.

Even more frightening was the great 1918–19 influenza epidemic that followed the war. The virus, which was brought home to the United States by returning troops, circled the world several times, killing as many as fifty million people. Although certain areas of the globe may be much better prepared today to cope with a new subtype virus, a virus deliberately engineered to have devastating consequences could easily be even more disastrous than the 1918–19 epidemic.

Today, it would be a relatively simple task to engineer a deadly disease that is extremely difficult to diagnose or treat; that could be unleashed across the entire United States, or Europe; and that would make it virtually impossible for the nation to go to war or defend itself. This could be done covertly yet quite effectively. The first signs would be a spiraling number of sick people, tens of millions within several days or a few weeks, which would almost immediately overwhelm existing health-care resources. Little imagination is required in the age of AIDS to appreciate how deadly a new virus can be and how its appearance can easily and quickly lead to mass hysteria.

Disease has always been the scourge of battle. During the Korean War, the rate of army casualties due to disease was ten times the rate of battle casualties. In the Vietnam War, over two-thirds of all army casualties were due to disease. In neither case were there any known enemy efforts to introduce unexpected diseases that would have been difficult to diagnose and treat, nor were there diseases that had been specifically made resistant to expected medical treatment. Either possibility could have had a catastrophic effect on U.S. military fighting-force effectiveness.

This is not science fiction. It is contemporary reality. Despite the threat, there is little appreciation in the United States of the scientific revolution that has taken place: not in the government, not in the military, and not in the scientific community. Most Americans still think in terms of the World War I use of chemicals on the battlefields of Europe. Only since the early 1980s have defense specialists begun to recognize the existence of new Soviet C/B weapons systems more effective than nerve agents. A few now even acknowledge that battlefield use would extend well beyond the front lines and would be exploited by well-trained Soviet and Eastern European troops. But aside from these exceptions, the situation envisioned by today's defense planners has not progressed much beyond the experiences of World War I.

Almost no attention is paid to the use of biological agents, the employment of C/B agents against civilian and political targets, the use of chemical agents that destroy the mind during "peacetime," or to the eventual use of C/B agents by terrorists and saboteurs.

One of the newest threats to emerge is that posed by terrorists of all varieties. And why not? C/B weapons are the essence of terror. They are, without question, the "poor man's atomic bomb." Should terrorists systematically begin to employ C/B agents, totally new vistas of terror would be possible. Terrorists are known to be informed and capable. The techniques and materials are readily available. Little is being done to prepare for this inevitable escalation of terror.

Since the beginning of the 1980s, C/B proliferation has become a major world problem. The chemical warfare genie is out of the bottle. This was the real message contained in the charges of mass employment of chemical weapons in Southeast Asia and Afghanistan. Though there remain a dwindling few who still refuse to confront the evidence in these two cases, none dispute the repeated use of mustard, phosgene, and nerve agents by Iraq in 1983–86 to stop invading Iranian forces. Countries throughout the Middle East are acquiring gas masks and protective gear as fast as they can; others are building their own chemical weapons capability; many are doing both. Proliferation is running rampant, yet there is little understanding of what it means or of how the United States should respond.

The event of greatest long-term significance is the biotechnology and genetic engineering revolution that began in the early 1970s. It is becoming recognized as the most significant technological event since the Industrial Revolution.

The scientific advances are so fascinating and their potential for understanding and improving the life processes are so exciting, that the dire consequences of their application to the black art of C/B warfare has gone almost unnoticed. These consequences are so great, that any biological, chemical, or medical scientist who considers the possibilities immediately recognizes that they are unlimited—and the consequences truly frightening. Almost no effort is required to reach those conclusions. The only question is: Which of the plethora of possibilities are the enemies of the United States likely to pursue? At present there is almost no recognition or understanding of the nature of the C/B warfare program that has been initiated by the Soviet Union, and efforts to achieve such an understanding have only recently begun.

A relatively recent phenomenon is the concern that the Soviet Union has been engaged, since the early 1970s, in an all-out effort to apply biotechnology and genetic engineering to create an entirely new family of C/B warfare agents. In 1984 the Defense Department reported that the first products of the Soviet effort already were being incorporated into their arsenal of C/B weapons. What are the new threats or risks to the United States and its allies among the offspring of the new Soviet technology? This is the critical uncertainty. Moreover, there is little comprehension of Soviet objectives and how they might affect U.S. security.

The most serious chemical warfare actually directed at the United States and Europe today is the deliberate marketing of drugs and narcotics intended to demoralize U.S. military forces and disrupt the social fabric of the United States. Early in the 1960s public concern began to rise over the problem of illegal drugs and narcotics in the United States. The Nixon administration in 1969 announced a major federal effort to address the problem. Results, however, were negligible. This has not kept each succeeding administration from calling for a new war on the flow of illegal drugs into the United States. Yet the problem not only persists: it has steadily worsened.

Unfortunately, it is only recently that there has been some realization in the West that this drug plague is not an accident, or simply the product of a variety of domestic social ills. Rather, it is in significant measure the consequence of a number of contributing factors, not the least of which is the direct role played by nations such as Cuba, Nicaragua, Bulgaria, East Germany, and Hungary. There is also a direct connection between the Western drug problem and communist-sponsored terrorism and revolutionary warfare. Still to emerge is an understanding of the role of the People's Republic of China (the largest opium producer in the world), and the Soviet Union (which stands behind and directs the intelligence services of its Eastern-bloc satellites, Cuba, and Nicaragua in their drug- and narcotics-pushing activities).

The drug and narcotics problem also is being revolutionized by advances in science and technology. Marijuana, hashish, opium, heroin, and cocaine—especially so-called "crack," the rapidly addictive form of cocaine—continue to be used and consumed in increasing amounts, but synthetic drugs have made significant inroads. Beginning with LSD in the late 1950s, then amphetamines in the 1960s, followed by barbiturates and methaqualone, synthetics have played an increasingly important role in the distribution chain. The real revolution, however, is yet to come: the so-called "designer drugs," which can be made to mimic heroin but are several thousand times more potent. The problem is rapidly becoming a true epidemic and proposed solutions that do not recognize and take into account the primary instigators and managers in the supply line and their objectives are unlikely to succeed.

The history of warfare has been inexorably linked to advances in science and technology, especially since the beginning of this century. The machine gun, tanks and airplanes, nuclear weapons, and intercontinental ballistic missiles have filled the arsenals of many nations and most have been used. Ever since chemical weapons were first used in 1915, there has always been the fear that C/B weapons would emerge as the "ultimate" weapons of war.

For half a century, the development and stockpiling of C/B agents has progressed, but their use, fortunately, has been contained until recently. Part of the reason they were not used was their newness and various uncertainties connected to their effects. Certainly there was the traditional concern by the major powers over maintaining control over the use of such weapons. No one wanted to be the first to use C/B weapons out of fear of possible retaliation. Irrespective of such reasons, the long-standing tradition of nonuse now has been broken in a series of Third World conflicts. It is important to note that in every instance, the agents have proven quite effective. Coupled with enormous advances in the underlying science, this raises the all-too-real specter of a new era of warfare, an era in which high-tech and widely disseminated biochem weapons will replace nuclear weapons as the chief scourge of mankind.

The question is, How should the United States respond to this emerging new threat? Certainly, the main and quite justified fear is that the United States will embark on a new and likely never-ending program to develop its own high-tech retaliatory capability. At present, about the only option that would be worse is to do nothing. But, there is a far more intelligent approach to take, and that begins with a effort to learn the true dimensions and sources of the problem. That understanding does not now exist and needs urgently to be developed.

The chapters that follow explore the various dimensions of the

C/B warfare problem and highlight the more obvious dangers. What ultimately makes the problem so serious is the combination of new scientific advances with the rapid proliferation of the technology horizontally (to other nations and cultures) and vertically (to lower educational levels).

Perhaps no single development is more representative of the problem than the advertisement of genetic engineering and gene cloning kits for children that appeared in the *Robb Report* during the 1985 Christmas season. Biochem warfare science and engineering are entering the mainstream of society around the world, and the question is, What is the United States prepared and willing to do?

Scenario One: Kafr Assad, West Bank

As the sun climbed slowly off the horizon, a light, steady wind from Jordan swept through the new West Bank settlement of Kafr Assad, rustling the leaves of the olive and acacia trees near the heart of the village. One of the six recently established Jewish settlements, Kafr Assad had been constructed, along with its sister enclaves, amidst a fresh firestorm of controversy. The Israeli government remained characteristically unwavering in the face of new U.S. threats to decrease military aid if Israel did not call a halt to the colonization of the West Bank.

Arab, African, and Eastern bloc governments were, as expected, unanimous in their denunciations of Israel, and European capitals competed to see which could heap the most invective on the government in Jerusalem. Only the PLO remained silent. Israeli intelligence analysts were mystified. Normally the various Palestinian revolutionary commands issued statements within hours of the announcement of new settlements. Then, just as the silence was becoming deafening, the long-awaited communiqué appeared.

The PLO announced that the establishment of Jewish settlements on Arab land had become intolerable and that it would not be permitted to go unchallenged any longer. "We will not yield an-

*other square meter of Arab land," affirmed the communiqué. "If
Israel does not begin at once to dismantle the six new settlements,
we will not be responsible for the consequences."*

*That was three weeks earlier. Construction of the new settle-
ments had proceeded on schedule, and Kafr Assad was beginning
to take shape. More than two dozen small houses had been completed. Shops, a school, and other community facilities were under
construction. For weeks, Kafr Assad had been a beehive of activity,
with construction equipment, noise, and dust everywhere. But today, as the truck carrying a load of building supplies wound its way
up the dusty road leading to Kafr Assad, the little settlement was
strangely quiet. There were no children, no activity, no dust.*

*As the truck approached the outer perimeter of the settlement,
which was ringed with coils of concertina wire, the driver braked
to a stop, jerking awake his companion who had been dozing in the
hot cab.*

"What is it?" mumbled Zvi Sharett.

*"I don't know," answered the driver, Danny Epstein, as he sur-
veyed the cluster of buildings less than a hundred yards distant. "It
doesn't look right. Where is everyone?"*

*"Beats me. There's probably a general meeting or something
going on."*

*They continued to observe the stark settlement for another
thirty seconds. Somewhere in the distance an unlatched door
banged rhythmically every few moments.*

*"You're probably right," said Danny, at last. As he eased the
truck forward, he reached down with his right hand and touched
the Uzi submachine gun, lying on the seat between them, for
reassurance.*

*The truck reached the first cluster of buildings, but there were
still no signs of life. Without warning, Danny stood on the brakes
again.*

"What's that up ahead in the road? It looks like a body."

"It s-sure does," agreed Zvi, fear welling up inside him.

"We'd better take a look."

"Yeah," replied Zvi, without conviction.

Danny grabbed the Uzi and jumped from the cab, leaving the truck idling in the middle of the road. Zvi pulled a pistol from inside his jacket and joined his companion. They moved into the shade cast by a row of sheds and scuttled along like rats, hunched over and close to the ground. When they reached the body, Danny covered Zvi as he stepped out into the bright sunlight and knelt down. The body was that of a young man in his mid-twenties, clad in an undershirt, khaki shorts, and military boots. A Galil rifle lay in the dirt nearby.

Zvi swatted at the flies and rolled the body over. The young man's face was a frozen mask of convulsive terror, his mouth and the front of his shirt caked with dried vomit, his lifeless eyes receded deeply into the skull.

"Well?" called Danny, his eyes scanning nearby rooftops for signs of trouble. "Was he shot?"

"I-I don't think so. There's no sign of any wound."

Zvi stood up shakily and a moment later followed Danny over to the construction site.

"Zvi, look over there," breathed Danny in disbelief.

A dozen men and women were sprawled about the site. Again, there were no wounds, no blood, no destruction. Everything looked normal except for the bodies and tools lying about and the cement hardening in the trough.

"I've seen enough," said Danny. "Let's head over to the com shack and get some help up here."

The settlement's headquarters and communication center was a one-story prefabricated building located a short distance away. Danny kicked open the door and burst in, the Uzi level and ready for action.

A pale white light seeped through the high, louvered windows; the headquarters looked more like a warehouse than an administrative center. Crates, boxes, tools, and household goods were stacked everywhere. In one corner, an attractive young woman was slumped over a desk, her long fingers still entwined around the handle of a full cup of coffee. Zvi remembered her from previous trips to Kafr Assad; she always signed the papers.

"Zvi!" Danny's urgent call derailed his companion's train of thought. Zvi joined Danny in the back room where the communications gear was located. Seated in front of a wireless, head back, mouth open, eyes rolled back in the sockets, was the camp administrator. He, too, was dead, apparently killed while in the process of making a call.

Danny stripped the headset from the dead man and handed it to Zvi. "Here, sound the alarm. I'll wait outside and stand guard."

Zvi slipped on the headset and began twisting dials.

A few minutes later he emerged from the building.

"Did you get hold of anyone?" inquired Danny eagerly.

Zvi dabbed at his nose, which had begun to run, and blinked his eyes to clear his vision. "Y-yeah, I raised a military post about ten kilometers from here. They're on the way." His chest felt tight, as though someone had him in a bear hug. Each breath was an effort.

"What is it?" Danny wanted to know, sensing his friend's distress.

Zvi could barely see; the light was receding in front of him like a slow fade in a movie. A wave of nausea passed over him and he was sweating like someone in a steambath.

"Zvi?" Danny's call sounded distant.

"W-what's happening to m-me?" Zvi cried. "What's . . . happening . . . to-o-o . . ."

His vision gone, his head disintegrating inside, he reached out to steady himself on the wall, but his legs turned to rubber and he collapsed in a heap, arms twitching wildly, gasping for breath, choking on the vomit rising in his throat.

Danny dragged his stricken companion back to the truck and pushed him into the cab. Minutes later, as he careened away from Kafr Assad, Danny vomited in his lap and slumped forward into the windshield. The truck went off the road and overturned in a ditch.

That evening in Jerusalem, a grim-faced spokesman for the Israeli government stepped in front of a sea of reporters and television crews and made a terse announcement:

"This morning, shortly after dawn, a deadly nerve agent was released upwind of the West Bank settlement of Kafr Assad. The entire village—fifty-three men, women, and children—was wiped out. A group calling itself the Justice Commandos of the Palestinian Revolution has claimed responsibility for the attack and has vowed further attacks unless Israel withdraws totally from the West Bank."

1
Bugs and Gas:
The New Technoterrorists

An Invitation to Terror

Welcome to the "brave new world" of terrorist violence, a world where the click of a camera shutter releases a deadly virus into a room; of death-dealing envelopes and postage stamps with a lethal toxin in the glue; of terrorist groups armed with C/B weapons capable of inflicting thousands of casualties without warning.

Although many observers have viewed the production of so-called fright weapons by terrorists as little more than science fiction, the chilling prospect of a terrorist group building or stealing C/B weapons is a very real threat. The development of C/B "Saturday night specials" is not technologically demanding and would be almost impossible to prevent. Any resourceful person with a college degree in chemistry or microbiology and access to fairly common raw materials could, in the privacy of a kitchen or garage, brew up a C/B weapon capable of wiping out thousands of innocent people. The possession of such a weapon would give terrorists the ability to blackmail the governments of states both large and small.

Perhaps the chief "fright scenario" to date involves terrorists somehow obtaining a nuclear bomb. Despite the popular fiction, television shows, and congressional speculation devoted to this theme, descriptions of terrorists constructing fissionable devices that work are so far-fetched as to be unworthy of serious attention at this time. The production of a nuclear device requires detailed knowledge and accurate instructions, elaborate laboratory and machining facilities, and—most difficult of all—fissionable material. Contrary to press speculation, there remain substantial gaps in the published data on the manufacture of nuclear weapons; key items in the inventory of laboratory and machining equipment are closely monitored by international authorities; and there is no known black market in fissionable material.

Although the prospect of Muammar Qaddafi obtaining a nuclear weapon is clearly disquieting, the more important point is that he has tried and failed. Moreover, consider Iraq, which has sought to develop a nuclear capability to counter Israel's since 1967. After efforts to enlist external assistance failed, Iraq decided to build its own indigenous nuclear capability, only to be stopped dead in its tracks in June 1981, when Israel bombed the Osirak nuclear reactor outside Baghdad. In view of the fact that most of the well-financed efforts by foreign nations to produce nuclear weapons have so far failed to win them admission to the nuclear club, little credibility can be attached to any scenario involving a handful of dissidents clandestinely building a bomb. Besides, the equally horrifying alternatives of C/B agents are so much easier, more cost-effective, and far less risky.

But what are we talking about when we refer to "chemical" and "biological" agents? The classic chemical agents can be classified in various ways, including by what they affect (blood, skin, or nerves) and the physical state in which they appear (gas, liquid, or solid). From a terrorist perspective, the more interesting agents are the widely advertised nerve agents, the organophosphorous compounds that have been described as "doing to humans what insect sprays do to insects." And, though the more sophisticated nerve agents are difficult and dangerous to manufacture, there are many varieties that are no more difficult to make than insect sprays and, subsequently, relatively easy to weaponize. Terrorist organizations can also bypass the manufacturing problem by simply purchasing suitable toxic chemicals such as parathion or phosgene that are readily available at many agricultural or industrial chemical supply stores.

Although chemical agents are generally cheaper, easier to use, and more containable than most biological agents, few of them (with the exception of nerve agents) have "a casualty producing potential comparable to that of biological agents," according to a World Health Organization report. Biological agents are the ultimate weapons of terror, whether in the possession of an advanced and powerful nation such as the Soviet Union, or in the arsenals of unstable rulers such as Libya's Colonel Qaddafi, a religious fanatic like the Ayatollah Khomeini, or just quietly growing in the bathtub at a terrorist safe house.

Biological agents are, in a word, microorganisms, too small to be seen with the naked eye. The largest are fungi and the smallest, viruses. In between are protozoa, bacteria, and rickettsiae. Among the most serious viral agents are those that produce dengue fever, Rift Valley fever, encephalitis, smallpox, yellow fever, and influenza. Typhus, Q fever, and Rocky Mountain spotted fever are rickettsial infections. Bacterial agents can induce the plague, tularemia, brucellosis, anthrax, and typhoid fever. From the standpoint of manufacturing biological weapons, a terrorist group would likely choose a bacteriological rather than viral or rickettsial agent. Rickettsial infections can be readily treated with antibiotics, and viruses are more difficult than bacteria to cultivate and often do not live long outside a host.

Toxins, in between the biological and chemical agents, are the poisonous by-products of microorganisms, plants, and animals. Toxins tend to be more stable than microorganisms because they are not living. Some toxins have the advantage, such as ricin and botulinus toxin, of being relatively simple to manufacture in a garage or basement, and of being extremely toxic—even more toxic than nerve agents on an equal-weight basis.

From the standpoint of weapons systems, chemical agents generally have been considered to be superior to either biological agents or toxins because of their stability, ease of manufacture and dispersal, and controllability (inasmuch as they are not contagious). The fact that they are not infectious is important to terrorists chiefly from the standpoint of safety. This is important both with respect to fellow members of their own community who may live in proximity to the intended victims of the attack, and to the fact that safe houses where the dangerous agents are grown and processed are likely to be located in areas or neighborhoods populated by support groups, coreligionists, or members of the same ethnic group or race.

Biological agents, by their very nature, are indiscriminate weapons, difficult to control or contain.

A good example of the control problem is found in German intelligence studies of Soviet biological warfare experiments prior to and during World War II. In 1941, the Soviets experimented on political prisoners in Ulan Bator and other parts of Mongolia. According to an intelligence study derived from hundreds of Soviet documents and prisoners captured during World War II: "The prisoners in chains were brought into an 8-man tent, on the floor of which under wire nets were kept rats infested with pest fleas; the latter transmit the infection to the subject of the experiment. The experiments were positive in most cases and the infection ended in bubonic plague." However, the report continues, some prisoners escaped and "started a great plague epidemic among the Mongols." Efforts to contain the spread of the disease were not successful until some three to five thousand Mongols had perished.

The biggest problem with C/B agents, especially biological ones, is how to efficiently deliver the payload (that is, the biological organisms) to the intended target. All biological agents require a biological delivery system or "vector." Distribution may be difficult if live animals or insects are required to deliver the agents. Because of their great lethality and dependence on winds and weather, the use of biological agents on the crowded West Bank by Palestinian terrorists, as described in scenario 1, would be an act of madness, and one as threatening to the indigenous Arab population and the surrounding Arab states as to the Jewish population. Thus, in the scenario, the terrorists opted for a chemical weapon (in this case, a nerve agent) that could be released upwind of the settlement. Based on the topography and weather conditions, and barring a shift in the direction of the wind, the results would be sufficiently predictable.

Nor are terrorists limited to the obvious C/B agents. If they choose, they can easily enter the uncharted waters of genetic tinkering, and manufacture chemical mutagens that interfere with genetic codes, or diseases that are resistant to any existing antibiotics and for which the body has no known defenses. They could even opt for psychochemical agents capable of producing profound behavioral changes in target populations. Certain drugs produce sexual dysfunctions, lethargy, and depression; still others have mind-altering characteristics that disrupt the ability to think logically, and therefore produce "psychological blindness." This is, after all, precisely what many of the new California drug dealers are doing: making their own "designer drugs" that are thousands of times more potent than the hard narcotics, such as heroin. Obviously terrorists could do the same thing. Such drugs, or "off-the-rocker" agents, could be surreptitiously administered to an unsuspecting population, with grave societal and national security consequences.

Why Would Terrorists Build a C/B Weapon?

Why would terrorists want to go beyond more conventional weapons and enter the realm of mass destruction weapons? Because the essence of terrorism is to intimidate and to sow fear, the most horrific and intimidating weapons are those capable of mass destruction: nuclear, chemical, and biological. As violence in the modern world becomes more and more routinized and commonplace, terrorists may strive to reach ever greater heights of terror to capture headlines and television time, and ultimately to force governments to do their will. Governments are as terrified of weapons of mass destruction as is the man on the street.

C/B weapons are the stuff of nightmares. Only nuclear weapons rival C/B weapons in conjuring up visions of the apocalypse. It should be recalled that the fear of chemical agents was used in the film *Close Encounters* to clear the mountain of all nonessential personnel. The sight of human tissue infected with anthrax (black leathery skin erupting with massive blisters) or the eerie stillness of the island of Gruinard, off the northwest coast of Scotland (still uninhabited more than thirty years after biological warfare tests were conducted), bear mute testimony to the horror of such weapons.

The very thought of an encounter with CX, or phosgene oxime, a Soviet blister agent, is enough to make cowards of even the most

hardened fighting men. Phosgene oxime is one of the agents suspected of being employed along with tricothecene mycotoxins in
Southeast Asia. Though it was one of the original chemical warfare
agents, it is now more widely known simply as a toxic industrial
chemical, and, as such, it is manufactured, stored, shipped, and sold
throughout the United States like dozens of other toxic chemicals.

Unlike many agents, CX produces immediate and horrible pain.
The affected skin blanches within seconds, and during the next half
hour an ugly sore forms. In the weeks that follow, a scab appears,
then the scab falls off leaving an ulcerating sore once again. The
sore may take several months to heal, during which time the victims
suffer excruciating pain. But what makes CX so insidious is that
even after the victims think they have fully recovered, the sore may
recur, even two or three times, up to a year after remission. These
consequences of exposure to CX led one expert to remark, "Suicide
could be the biggest cause of death from CX."

There are many practical reasons why C/B weapons would
prove attractive to terrorist groups. First of all, they are cheap—
C/B weapons are "the poor man's atomic bomb." A sophisticated
program designed to produce a fissionable device would probably
cost hundreds of millions of dollars, whereas type A botulinus
toxin, which is more deadly than nerve gas, could be produced
for about $400 per kilogram. A group of C/B experts, appearing
before a UN panel in 1969, estimated "for a large-scale operation
against a civilian population, casualties might cost about $2,000
per square kilometer with conventional weapons, $800 with nu-
clear weapons, $600 with nerve-gas weapons, and $1 with biological weapons."

Second, C/B weapons can be produced without much difficulty
and in a relatively short time. Such weapons could be built clandestinely by individuals of moderate educational attainment with only
a minimum of tools and space. Nearly all of the equipment needed
could be improvised or purchased without arousing suspicion. For-
mulas for manufacturing nerve agents, mustard gas, LSD, and herbicides are readily available in various scientific texts. In 1971, the
Defense Department itself declassified the formula for VX, its most
potent nerve agent. A publication entitled, *C-Agents: Properties
and Protection,* produced by the Swedish Armed Forces Research

Institute, even describes in detail how to launch a gas attack, including formulae for calculating wind speed and lethal concentrations of the agent.

Nevertheless, terrorists and other malefactors run clear risks in attempting to produce C/B agents. The same inherent qualities that make C/B agents attractive instruments of terror can backfire and inflict death or suffering on the careless or ill-informed amateur engaged in their manufacture. Published chemical formulae and instructions are often inadequate because the so-called "alchemist's art" is deliberately left out. These are the tricks that are often so essential to obtain a proper product. Some instructions are even published with deliberate "errors" included—slight errors in quantity, or temperature, or process that have been sophisticatedly designed to cause serious problems for the amateur, or more specifically, for the untrained terrorist.

Third, only a very small amount of a C/B agent represents a real threat. The amount of VX (a nerve agent) that one can place on the head of a pin is sufficient to produce death in a human being. Four tons of VX is enough to cause several hundred thousand deaths if released in aerosol form in a crowded urban area. It would take only fifty kilograms (slightly over one hundred pounds) of anthrax spores in aerosol form to produce an equivalent number of casualties. Only a minute quantity of many biological agents is enough to infect a victim. For example, although Q fever is not as dangerous as many diseases from the standpoint of mortality rates, it is extremely infectious. Only a few organisms are enough to produce the disease in a human being. Because of its high infectivity, Q fever is especially dangerous. Working with two dozen chicken eggs and high-school level technology, a terrorist could brew up a quart of Q fever organisms, or literally billions of infective doses. And, though there are bound to be gross inefficiencies associated with any delivery mechanism, a truck or car equipped with a cheap commercial aerosolizer, such as used to spray trees and plants, would pose a major threat to a large city or seat of government.

Fourth, virtually any target is vulnerable to a C/B attack. Even the shelter underneath the White House and the command centers in the Pentagon, which have air and water filtration systems, have reportedly flunked simulated studies and mock C/B attacks by spe-

cial "black hat" military teams. "There is no question," according
to a former Secret Service agent, "but that you could introduce
something of a toxic nature into the White House water. While the
water is monitored and watched for content, the technique is not
foolproof." U.S. cities, moreover, are all but defenseless to a C/B
attack; civil defense planners have done little more than wring their
hands at the prospect.

Given this extremely poor state of preparedness, should such an
attack occur, it is unlikely that it could be rapidly detected or that
the specific agent would be expeditiously identified. A good example of this problem is an event that took place in spring 1983 when
a truck accidentally spilled a bulk container of talcum powder on
the San Francisco–Oakland Bay Bridge. The truck driver continued
on his way, presumably unaware of the spillage. Traffic in the Bay
Area was snarled for roughly eight hours while authorities worked
to discover the nature of the "contaminant." Few police departments or civil defense units have standard U.S. military chemical
agent detector kits or such things as detector paper and vesicant
detector crayons, and there are no simple detectors for toxins and
biological agents.

Fifth, as previously noted, C/B weapons pose far less of a hazard
than attempting to build a nuclear weapon. Not only can a C/B
device be manufactured without arousing undue suspicion, but it
can be applied covertly, allowing the terrorists ample opportunity
to get away before the attack is discovered. Dissemination of the
agent can be easily disguised, with the exception of dispersal methods using explosives.

Sixth, C/B weapons, by comparison to fissionable devices, are
characterized by a high degree of reliability. Because of the inability
to test it, any terrorist-built nuclear bomb would stand a high probability of being a dud. A C/B device, on the other hand, could be
field-tested with only moderate risk to the security of the project.
Special chambers, certain sampling gear, and test animals would be
necessary. Disposal of the test animals' carcasses would be the risk-
iest procedure. Most terrorists would probably not do extensive
testing, but simply rely on overkill. Alternatively, on-the-job research might be more than adequate. Mix up a brew and try it out.

If it fails, back to the test tubes. If it works, claim the credit and warn the authorities of what lies ahead if demands are not met.

Scenario Two: Lawrence, Kansas

It was just after midnight. Four technicians at the Lawrence, Kansas, municipal waterworks were sitting around a long Formica-topped table drinking coffee when the door leading to the main hall was kicked open with a bang, revealing a ski-masked intruder with an Armalite assault rifle.

"Everyone on their feet," barked the intruder. "And hands in the air."

One man leaped up, overturning his coffee cup. Two others rose slowly, but one man simply stared at the intruder in disbelief. The masked man sprayed a burst from his weapon into the ceiling.

"I said get up! Everyone against the wall."

This time the orders were obeyed without protest or delay. The four frightened technicians lined up against the wall. Without warning, the intruder opened up with the Armalite, cutting them down in cold blood.

Seconds later, two more ski-masked intruders entered the room, one wheeling a fifty-five-gallon drum on a dolly. While the man with the Armalite stood guard outside, his two companions shut down the water purification and pollution detection system and began introducing the contents of the drum into the water system, but not before donning overboots, gloves, bulky protective clothing, and respirator hoods.

Over the next six hours the deadly contents of the drum were slowly released into the sleeping city's water mains. At 6:00 A.M., two hours before the daytime shift at the waterworks was scheduled to report for duty, the terrorists slipped away in a dark-colored van, leaving behind the bodies of the four technicians.

Two hours later, the first symptoms began to appear in residents of the community. Local hospitals received calls from people complaining of debilitating weakness, dizziness, blurred vision, and cotton mouth. At 8:30 A.M., only minutes after the massacre at the waterworks was discovered, an emergency case arrived at the city hospital with partial facial paralysis and respiratory difficulty. Thirty minutes later, he was dead, the victim of cardiac arrest. The corpse was still on its way down to autopsy when another case, nearly identical to the first one, was wheeled from an ambulance into the emergency room.

As the emergency room staff tried desperately to save the twenty-five-year-old woman's life, a nurse in admitting collapsed. It was at that moment that Dr. Robert Trammel picked up the phone and dialed the state health authorities.

An aura of crisis hung over the White House that evening. At 9:40 P.M., nearly twenty-one hours after the deadly agent had first been introduced into the Lawrence water system, the president and his chief advisors were cloistered in the Situation Room. The White House press room, which usually was deserted by that hour—most correspondents would have filed their stories and gone home or had slipped behind a martini someplace along Seventeenth Street—was packed to the rafters with reporters clamoring for an official statement concerning the crisis. Television cameras were set up on the White House lawn and across Pennsylvania Avenue in Lafayette Park.

Bathed in the soft green light of the Situation Room, the National Security Advisor was beginning his briefing. He had a small, squat face perched atop a thick neck. He was bald except for a fringe of closely trimmed hair that formed a horseshoe around his head; his face was dominated by a pair of thick, tinted, plastic-framed spectacles. When he spoke, his heavy arched eyebrows seemed to float up and down on his forehead with a life of their own.

Sucking in his stomach and straightening up in his chair, he surveyed the solemn faces gathered around the table.

"As you know," he began matter-of-factly, folding his hands and speaking to the assembled officials in much the same manner he used to address students in his graduate seminar, "this group was established to deal with national security threats from terrorists employing biologicals, nerve agents, nuclear weapons, and other weapons of mass destruction." He lowered his voice; his words tip-

toed through the room. Those around the table leaned forward in their chairs, straining to hear. He licked the corners of his mouth, then continued, slowly, without emotion. "Well, what we all prayed would never happen has happened. Gentlemen, there has been a 'Top Event.'"

A noticeable stir passed among the group.

"At approximately midnight, Central time, an unknown number of terrorists seized the Lawrence, Kansas, waterworks. They murdered four employees, shut down the monitoring and filtration systems, and began dumping a deadly poison into the water."

"Have we identified the poison yet?" someone asked.

"Yes, it was type A botulinus toxin. For those of you unfamiliar with botulinus toxin, let me just say that it is just about the most poisonous substance known, so deadly, in fact, that something like eight ounces, properly dispersed, could wipe out the entire world population. To put its toxicity into perspective, the amount needed to kill one human being can be likened to a flea on a hundred-mile-long train, the flea's presence being able to derail the whole train."

"That's unbelievable," muttered the President, sitting with his hands clasped before his face, both thumbs rocking against his teeth.

"The bodies of the murdered employees were discovered around 8:00 A.M.," continued the National Security Advisor, "yet it took nearly three hours for local authorities to decide to close down the water system. The first bulletins warning the residents not to drink or come in contact with the water did not appear on the radio and TV until nearly noon. By then, it was too late. According to estimates supplied by me by Dr. Clausen, Director of the Centers for Disease Control in Atlanta, nearly 60 percent of the residents of Lawrence probably ingested lethal doses of the agent before remedial action was begun."

Shock registered on the faces of all assembled.

"That's something like twenty-five or thirty thousand deaths," gasped the Director of the FBI.

"I . . . know," answered the National Security Advisor gravely. "We are doing everything possible to aid the victims. Lawrence is being evacuated by the army. Casualties—I think we have nearly *fifteen thousand people showing symptoms at last report—are being airlifted to special emergency treatment centers at hospitals and military bases around the country."*

"How about communication with the terrorists?" asked the President. "Have we heard from them yet? Have any demands been conveyed to the government?"

"No, not yet. But we assume it's only a matter of time before we hear from them."

"Have we a clue as to who might be behind the attack?" pressed the President.

The National Security Advisor shook his head. "No."

"This is terrible business," reflected the President. His face was heavily lined and sagging with the strain of the crisis. "You know, I've been asking people how this could happen and they all tell me that it's damn near impossible to protect the country from things like this. All we can do, they say, is react when the worst happens. Now that's no way to run a government, is it? We've got to do better in the future, gentlemen. Got to do better."

How Easy Is It to Build a C/B Weapon?

According to a recent study by the BDM Corporation, the "ideal" requirements for manufacturing a fairly sophisticated biological weapon include one microbiologist with knowledge of disease processes; one engineer; one vegetative bacterial pathogen; a microbiology laboratory; a bottle production plant; sterilizer capacity for the bottle production plant; and shop space and equipment. In addition, accurate formulae, a dispersing device and a detailed plan of attack are needed.

Though even these requirements are not particularly formidable, knowledgeable experts say that a resourceful terrorist group could cut corners and build a "no frills" weapon even more easily. They note that only a minimum of space is needed and that fairly rudimentary tools will suffice. Nearly everything that cannot be bought can be improvised. The laboratory could be easily concealed and the actual manufacture of weapons would be unlikely to attract attention. Small-scale testing could be undertaken with minimum risk; large-scale testing would be another matter. Whereas chemical weapons require a "moderately advanced chemical technique," the raw materials for a biological weapon are readily accessible in most countries and should present little difficulty to terrorists.

A culture of a pathogenic agent needed to manufacture a biological weapon could be obtained from a variety of sources. Many pathogenic agents. (including those that produce anthrax, the plague, brucellosis, tularemia, and smallpox) can be isolated from natural sources which, of course, are ultimately the source of all such agents. In the northern United States, corn is an excellent source of tricothecene mycotoxin, and in the south, aflatoxin can be produced from peanuts. Ricin toxin, which is over a thousand times more potent than the most advanced nerve agents, can be made from castor beans.

To grow their own pathogens, the would-be terrorists simply need to know where to look; a suitable growth medium is required, as are basic safety measures, and some testing is desirable. The literature describing various toxins and biological poisons is unclassified and amply detailed. To a knowledgeable person the procedures required to obtain strains or cultures of very dangerous toxins and diseases—and to produce them in sufficient quantities—are about as complicated as manufacturing beer and less dangerous than refining heroin. Viral and rickettsial agents could be grown in fertilized hen eggs, for example. Though ignoring the delivery problem, one study states that "theoretically, using a dozen chicken eggs in this fashion, enough psittacosis virus could be produced to infect everyone on earth." This provides a good description of the rather small production necessities.

The creation of a production capability that could produce large, harvestable amounts of many agents is time-consuming, but not technologically demanding. The drying and processing of the agent, and the development of dispersal devices, are more sophisticated tasks, but by no means prohibitively difficult. According to the World Health Organization study, some agents (such as smallpox virus) "can be produced and used as weapons with relatively simple techniques."

For example, to obtain a potent mixture of tricothecene mycotoxins, the terrorist need only make a slurry of corn meal, add contaminated corn or a strain of the appropriate fungus. The mixture would be put together with nutrients and an antibiotic such as streptomycin to increase the growth rate and yield. Then, the terrorist just sits back and lets the toxin-producing mold grow. At the appropriate time, the mixture is dried, ground, and the tricothecenes extracted with alcohol. The alcohol is then permitted to evaporate. The residue is a potent mixture of a wide variety of tricothecene mycotoxins, more potent than any one individual strain by itself. It is nearly as potent as a nerve agent if aflatoxin (made from peanuts) is added. Indeed, this is one of many advantages of toxins: Purity is not desired. The unpurified mixture, which may contain up to thirty-seven different mycotoxins, is more potent than a pure strain. And the only protections required in the manufacturing process are surgical gloves and a mask.

In the case of biological agents, terrorists need not waste time and effort isolating pathogenic agents from natural sources, although that is certainly one approach. A number of shortcuts exist, the most obvious being the theft of deadly cultures from a university or research foundation engaged in either medical or biological research. A terrorist posing as a graduate student or medical researcher involved in the field of epidemiology would likely have access to numerous pathogenic cultures that could be stolen with little effort or fear of exposure. A knowledgeable terrorist might even seek to obtain a disease strain resistant to anticipated methods of treatment. Medical and research personnel could also be blackmailed into turning pathogens over to terrorist cells. Most laboratories engaged in biological or related medical research have inadequate physical security, and little screening of personnel is routinely conducted.

The alarming fact is that marijuana is more closely regulated in the United States than access to and distribution of most deadly biological cultures. Cultures of most biological agents can be obtained from commercial medical supply laboratories. There is some control; a permit is required, but this is largely a formality to ensure that the recipient or laboratory is equipped to handle the material. Moreover, an Agriculture Department permit (rather than a public health permit) is required, because the principal concern is that of plant or animal infestation. To obtain a permit, it is only necessary to describe the recipient facility. If the facility meets the test of respectability, the bugs or fungi are available for a nominal fee.

Professional trade journals routinely carry advertisements for cultures of pathogenic agents: freeze-dried, packaged to facilitate laboratory use, and available through the mail. The only stated requirement is that the company providing the cultures must have reason to believe the recipient is appropriately trained and has the proper laboratory facilities to safely handle the pathogens. An acceptable letterhead, and a description of the type of work to be performed and the equipment available, should suffice.

A terrorist group could easily steal or forge a letterhead or develop a fictitious one capable of deceiving the personnel at one of the culture collection institutes or medical supply laboratories. Virtually any bacillus can be ordered from laboratories listed by the American Type Culture Collection (ATCC) of Rockville, Maryland, including *Bacillus anthracis* (anthrax) and the bacillus that produces botulinus toxin. And the cost of most of the specimen cultures is less than the cost of a handgun. *Bacillus anthracis* specimens cost about $35. One supply house, promoting the "sale" of five toxins for the price of four, offered five sample toxins, including T2 toxin (the so-called Yellow Rain in Afghanistan), for $100. Some years ago, a Japanese company sold tetrodotoxin in powdered form for $5.97 per gram.

Though simply ordering a pathogenic organism through the mail may seem improbable to many of us who have grown accustomed to living in a safe and secure environment, this is precisely what happened in the spring of 1984. Two Canadians, for reasons that are still unknown, crossed the border and called the ATCC from Buffalo. Posing as research microbiologists, they placed an order over the phone, requesting cultures of *Clostridium tetani* and *Clostridium septicum*. They gave the reputable firm of ICM Science as their affiliation, and requested the cultures be sent care of Federal Express in Cheektowaga, New York. A money order was sent and the ATCC promptly dispatched the cultures. As a matter of routine, ATCC sent a copy of the invoice to ICM Science. ICM Science recognized that it had not ordered the cultures and had no employees by the names given, and called the Canadian police and notified the ATCC. Shortly thereafter, the two individuals placed another order, this time for *Clostridium botulinum,* and the ATCC notified the FBI. This time, the perpetrators were caught when they arrived to pick up the package, which contained dummy cultures. Had ICM Science been less observant, both orders would have been filled and no one would have been alerted.

Direct-mail order is an obvious approach to obtaining desired cultures. But there are other methods that are far less public and hence preferable to terrorists. As researchers in the field know, there are no controls over the use of bugs by the recipient researcher or institution, except those that are self-imposed. The only federal controls are those associated with animal or human testing. There are some containment requirements for high-risk experiments in the area of genetic engineering, but in general no one really knows what anyone else is doing, or is particularly concerned. There would be little problem for "graduate student" conducting "research" to obtain cultures from a supply house or from other researchers. Culture swapping is a common practice, and largely uncontrolled.

Similarly, university laboratories conducting research with dangerous cultures police themselves, and standards vary greatly from one university to another. Because of the suspicion of law-enforcement authorities characteristic of many academics, it is questionable whether thefts or misuse of pathogens would be reported. According to the BDM study, Dr. C. Don Cox, chairman of the public affairs committee of the American Society of Microbiology, expressed his belief that university personnel would probably not report improperly documented requests for deadly cultures to law-enforcement officials. Furthermore, U.S. laboratories are not the only source of extremely dangerous viruses and bacteria. Scientists throughout the world conduct research using highly infectious and deadly microbes, often under even less secure conditions than in the United States.

And if terrorists could not obtain deadly microbes by more conventional routes, they could turn to patron nations for help. There is concern that this may already be happening. If this is so, this must be regarded as a serious and frightening threat to Western security.

Scenario Three: Hahn Air Force Base, West Germany

The Mercedes dumptruck carrying a load of sand wound its way through the narrow German streets toward the sprawling U.S. air base. It did not attract any special attention, as similar trucks were coming and going from a construction site near the air base, where a block of new apartments was rising.

It had rained earlier in the morning and the road still glistened with water in places, although the sun was beginning to break through the overcast. The young man behind the wheel of the truck glanced anxiously into his rearview mirror to see if anyone was following him and, satisfied that all was as it should be, he lit a cigarette and tried to relax.

As he approached the air base, he turned onto a broad boulevard that ran parallel to the outer edge of the facility. He took one last drag from the cigarette and tossed the butt out the window, eyes searching the road for the black BMW sedan containing his confederates. Suddenly he spotted the BMW, up ahead, parked near the curbside. As he passed by, the BMW pulled into traffic behind the dumptruck, staying well back.

The outside perimeter of the air base was surrounded by a chainlink fence topped with concertina wire. Long storage sheds and hangars obstructed the driver's view of the runways, but he could hear the fighter planes taking off on their routine exercises. When he reached a predesignated point on the boulevard, he steadied the wheel of the truck with his left hand and with his right twisted the handle on a small plastic box in his lap with wires trailing away through the back of the cab into the sand-filled tender of the truck.

There were several flashes of white light. The entire truck shuttered violently and was engulfed in smoke momentarily. The noise was so loud that the driver, despite his preparations and training, nearly jumped through the windshield. The truck moved to the right, striking several cars, while sand rained down on the scene. The black BMW gunned its engine, raced around the remains of several violent collisions involving other traffic on the boulevard, and pulled alongside the dumptruck as it screeched to a halt. The driver, still stunned and reeling, staggered out of the cab and was pulled into the BMW, which sped down the boulevard. It turned down a sidestreet a few blocks away, where a switch of vehicles took place.

The nine homemade mortar tubes buried in the sand had fired almost simultaneously, each launcher sending a mortar round containing five kilograms of a V-series nerve agent at the flight line. Eight of the nine rounds burst on impact, turning the toxic agent into a fine mist that enveloped a large area of the base including the tower, administration buildings, hangars, and workshops. An F-16 taxiing down the runway had been hit by one of the rounds and careened into several parked aircraft, whereupon it exploded in a large fireball.

The nerve agent cut down men and women almost in mid-stride as they darted through the smoke and confusion. Some would suddenly stumble and collapse in a pile of twitching limbs and vomit; others grasped their throats and toppled over like toy soldiers. One officer, screaming a dry hollow scream, jammed a syringe of atropine—a nerve gas antidote—into his thigh and sat down on the tarmac watching the melee with a dazed look on his face. Other victims, disoriented and choking, ran into the path of screaming firetrucks where they, too, were cut down.

Some of the deadly agent was carried by the breeze in a southerly direction, where it settled over a neighborhood of low-income housing abutting the air base, an unexpected bonus for the terrorists who had decided once again to show the Americans how really vulnerable they were. A woman, in the process of hanging clothes on a line, crashed face-forward into her laundry basket. Her neighbor had just arrived in a car and, when she opened the car door, pulled the deadly mist into her lungs, slumping forward onto the steering wheel, setting off the car horn, its noisy complaint echoing through the now still neighborhood. Several blocks away, more than a hundred children were at play in a schoolyard when they began to feel the effects of the agent. Within seconds, all were dead or dying.

How Serious Is the Threat?

According to one military planner familiar with the terrorist threat, "Bugs and drugs are the wave of the future." The threat of terrorists developing a C/B weapon and using it within the borders of the United States is so real that five years ago the Centers for Disease Control were asked to provide special assistance to the FBI antiterrorist special operations team. It was neither excessive paranoia nor overzealousness that motivated the request, but a series of alarming incidents involving the malevolent use of chemical and biological substances. Swimming pools have been poisoned in California; supermarket products have been laced with cyanide; terrorists have tried to poison urban water systems; railway cars in Austria were contaminated with radioactive iodine; and in Paris, authorities uncovered a terrorist laboratory engaged in the manufacture of a deadly biological poison.

The Paris incident is a good example of the problem. On 14 October 1984, Paris police raided a West German Red Army Faction (RAF) safe house at 41A Chaillot Street. The sixth-floor apartment contained typed sheets on bacterial pathology. Marginal notes were identified by graphologists as being the handwriting of Silke Maier-Witt, a medical assistant by profession, terrorist by night. Other items included medical publications dealing with the struggle against bacterial infection; printing presses; forged documents; rubber stamps; passports; and a cabinet filled with instructions for making bombs. In the bathroom, the French authorities found a bathtub filled with flasks containing cultures of *Clostridium botulinum*.

Of all the countries of the world, Israel is probably the most concerned, best protected, and extensively prepared to cope with terrorist C/B warfare. However, not withstanding the known Israeli attention to detail, their protective shield was penetrated in a still-secret 1984 chemical warfare incident in which the nerve agent carbamate was added to the coffee at an Israeli military mess.

One of the most serious attacks ever mounted against Israel by Palestinian terrorists occurred in 1978 and had a chemical dimension. Europeans in at least three countries became ill from eating Israeli citrus products—oranges, lemons, and grapefruit—that had been contaminated with mercury, which presumably had been injected under the skins of the citrus products with a syringe. A group identifying itself as the Arab Revolutionary Army Palestinian Commandos, in a letter to the Dutch government, announced that its goal was "to sabotage the Israeli economy." No one died from the incident and only slightly more than a dozen people were poisoned, but Israel's citrus exports were profoundly affected, with the loss of badly needed foreign exchange. Had additional attacks against Israel's fragile economy been carried out by the Palestinians, the impact could have been devastating.

A similar effort to contaminate fruit occurred in the Philippines, where Huk terrorists poisoned pineapples destined for the export market. The plot, however, was discovered and the contaminated pineapples were destroyed before they could harm anyone. The whole incident was then hushed up before it affected sales.

The use of C/B warfare reportedly has been discussed at terrorist meetings in Rome, Paris, and at several locations in West Germany. And, within the United States, the Symbionese Liberation Army flirted with the use of C/B weapons: The group used cyanide-dipped bullets, and authorities discovered military manuals on biological warfare in one of their safe houses.

Federal officials are still troubled by a 1974 incident. Authorities received a series of taped messages from an anonymous individual, who was known as the "Alphabet Bomber," threatening that the "Aliens of America" would take over the U.S. government if his demands were not heeded. In one of the messages, the Alphabet Bomber said that he possessed nerve gas and was coming to Washington to kill the president. According to those engaged in the Alphabet Bomber's apprehension, his description of the nerve agent was "highly sophisticated. He said all the right things and used the right pronunciations of extremely technical terms."

As a result, authorities were convinced that there was a "high probability" that the threat was real. From a room in the basement of the White House, the Secret Service and other federal law-enforcement officials coordinated one of the most intensive manhunts

in the nation's history. Using sophisticated audio equipment provided by the CIA, extensive psychological profiling, and a thorough
review of federal personnel records, the search was narrowed to a
single individual in Los Angeles. So effective was the commitment
of federal resources that the entire search took only eighteen hours.
And when the police apprehended the suspect, he was determined
to be the Alphabet Bomber. Originally from Yugoslavia, Muharem
Kerbegovic was arrested in connection with several other bomb-
ings. He had also sent toxic material through the mail to at least
one Supreme Court justice. Whether or not he had finished assembling the nerve agent is still an issue. Some reports suggest that he
had. Others maintain that he had assembled all but one of the critical ingredients, and that he had made arrangements to pick up the
remaining substance on the afternoon he was arrested.

Details are not available, but law-enforcement officials report
that this was not the only arrest in recent years where a C/B agent
was involved. Fortunately, most incidents purportedly involving
C/B agents have turned out to be hoaxes designed to extort ransom.
During the early 1970s, the Secret Service received a real scare when
an unidentified piece of metal marked "Porton Down," the British
C/B research center in Wiltshire, washed up on the beach near President Nixon's Key Biscayne retreat. It turned out to be a piece of
overpack which had been wrapped around the bomblets in a British
chemical munition. Although the British denied the existence of
such a weapon, it was traced to open-air tests they were conducting
in the Bahamas.

A more serious incident occurred in the Northeast in 1983. An
informer, in return for immunity from prosecution relating to a different crime, directed the FBI to a house in Springfield, Massachusetts, where two brothers were busily manufacturing the toxin ricin.
On an equal-weight basis, ricin is over a thousand times more toxic
than the U.S. nerve agent VX. The FBI seized the two, who had in
their possession an ounce of nearly pure ricin in a 35-mm film canister. The FBI agent put the canister inside an empty paint can and,
together with an EPA colleague, drove to MIT in Cambridge where
they learned from an expert what they had seized. Their next problem was how to dispose of the material. After conferring with sev-

eral specialists, they took the material under heavy police escort to the army's infectious disease laboratory at Ft. Detrick, Maryland, where it was first analyzed and then destroyed.

There are several suspected cases of biological terrorism, but proof is hard to come by. An interesting potential incident, currently under investigation, took place in Oregon in September 1984, in the region where Bhagwan Shree Rajneesh established his commune. Beginning on 15 September, citizens in the nearby town of Antelope became ill with salmonella poisoning. Within ten days, there were sixty clinical cases, all with the same strain, *Salmonella typhimurium*. Four different restaurants were involved, but there was no natural common source for the common strain. This gave rise to the conclusion that deliberate contamination was involved. One year later, in the squabble that emerged when his close personal aide Ma Anand Sheela fled the camp, Bhagwan charged that she had, among other things, "poisoned a nearby town."

One of the main reasons little is heard about terrorist interest in C/B warfare is that authorities are either totally ignorant of the subject or, conversely, so frightened by the implications of such disclosures that they suppress available evidence of C/B incidents perpetrated by terrorists and other nonstate actors. As but one illustration, the International Association of Chiefs of Police published a request in its newsletter in 1984 for any data available on C/B incidents. Their purpose was to analyze the data and develop a handbook for use in educating law-enforcement officials about the nature of the crime, its indicators, dangers, and developing approaches. They did not receive a single response! So they reran the notice, and again received no responses. It was as though the possibility had never existed. Yet, the known incidents that have been reported in the media exceed a dozen, and experts state that the real number is over three times that many.

The Soviet Union and its allies regularly accuse the United States of using C/B weapons covertly, most likely as a red herring to cover up their own promiscuous use of such weapons. Fidel Castro has repeatedly sought to explain Cuban sugarcane and other crop failures by accusing the United States of "germ warfare." Similarly, the Soviet news agency Tass recently claimed that the CIA was responsible for an outbreak of dengue fever in India and that the U.S. Air

Force was responsible for the mysterious pneumonia-like epidemic that struck Madrid in April 1981, near the U.S. airbase at Torrejón where (according to Soviet disinformation) U.S. biological agents were stored. One KGB-backed newspaper in Greece even headlined one fatuous report, "The CIA Trains Mosquitoes to Poison Populations—The Secrets of the CIA's Biological War."

According to materials provided by the CIA to the Senate Select Committee on Intelligence Activities during the mid-1970s, the CIA did develop "methods and systems for carrying out a covert attack against crops and causing severe crop loss." However, the CIA denied ever employing such systems, and there is no evidence that they ever used herbicides or biological agents against the crops of another nation. The Senate investigation into the activities of the CIA revealed that the agency had stockpiled at least fifteen deadly biological poisons and developed a number of weapons to deliver the lethal substances. Although the development of assassination weapons is now prohibited, the U.S. government has proceeded with efforts to create new incapacitating agents designed to overcome the enemy without lasting effect. Such substances might be particularly useful in hostage situations where indiscriminate gunfire aimed at "taking out the terrorists" might injure the hostages. Such weapons are also absolutely quiet, whereas even a sound-suppressed pistol has a muffled report. The U.S. commandos on the rescue mission to Tehran in 1980 are believed to have carried a chemical spray designed to be used in overpowering the guards at the U.S. Embassy compound. The spray lowers the blood pressure, and with any rapid movement, the individual who has been sprayed blacks out.

In what must surely be one of the most alarming developments in recent years, there is mounting evidence that the USSR is now passing on C/B warfare technology and materials to terrorist groups that support Moscow's international policy aims. Soviet documents captured from PLO bunkers in Lebanon in 1982 leave little doubt that there are connections between the USSR and the training of Third World countries and revolutionaries in the use of so-called chemical weapons, which is how toxins are most often categorized in Soviet military manuals. Cuba has also been reported to be a supply source for toxin and chemical weapons. South African intelligence sources report that members of the marxist-dominated

South West Africa People's Organization (SWAPO), fighting in Namibia, have received training in C/B warfare from Cuba and the PLO. Soviet policy sanctions the use of all possible means in supporting "revolutionary causes," and there is a strong link between special-force operations (*spetsnaz*) buttressing international terrorism, and so-called wet operations (assassinations), both of which are managed within the same directorates responsible for strategic intelligence operations in the KGB and GRU.

The Soviet Union, however, is not alone in making ill-considered transfers of deadly C/B substances to unstable countries. There are reports that France has provided Libya's erratic Colonel Qaddafi with a ton of the nerve agent Tabun (GA). However, Qaddafi's fascination with weapons of mass destruction is far from satiated. In view of Libya's failure, to date, to acquire a nuclear capability, the so-called "Moslem bomb" trumpeted by Qaddafi is far more likely to be a C/B weapon than a fissionable one. Indeed, there is every evidence today that Libya is currently engaged in an extensive, ongoing effort to develop chemical, and possibly even biological, weapons of mass destruction. Libyan operatives were recently arrested in the United States attempting to illegally purchase portable sterile environment equipment that could be used in the manufacture of biological warfare agents. Nor is the problem confined to governments. Non-U.S. industrial firms are known to have built chemical weapon turnkey plants in Third World countries with close terrorist links. At the same time, it is worth recalling that Western firms, mainly U.S. and West German firms, played a major role in the development of Soviet chemical warfare capabilities in the 1920s and 1930s.

Scenario Four: Richmond, Virginia

It started as a routine police call on a house in a working-class neighborhood in Richmond, Virginia, that served as the headquarters of a local religious cult. As two police officers approached the house with a warrant for the arrest of one of the cult members on bad-check charges, they were met by a barrage of gunfire. Both

*officers were hit, but one of them managed to reach the squad car
and radio for help.*

*The incident ended six hours later, after a shoot-out that left
three members of the cult and one police officer dead. Four other
police officers were wounded along with three cult members, and
five cultists were taken into custody. Inside the house, police discovered dozens of automatic weapons and a library of bomb-mak-
ing and mayhem manuals.*

*"Hey fellas, get a look at this," whistled Lieutenant Pete Buel
as he pulled back a tarpaulin, revealing a Chinese-made RPG-2 an-
titank missile launcher. As those nearby gathered around for a look,
Buel was summoned down into the cellar by one of his men, Officer
Leonard Washington.*

*Washington was stirring the ashes in an old coal-burning fur-
nace. Along one wall was a row of small cages, all empty but for
one in which cowered a mangy brown dog.*

*"Look at this, Lieutenant," called Washington, motioning Buel
closer. "It's full of bones. What do you think these freaks have been
doing?"*

*"I don't know," replied Buel, looking around the room. "What's
behind that door over there?" he asked, jerking his head in the direction of a closed door leading off to one side.*

"Beats me. I ain't been in there yet," responded Washington.

*Buel drew his service revolver and pushed on the door, which
swung slowly open. He reached around the corner and turned on
the light. While Washington covered him, he stepped into what appeared to be a laboratory of some kind. It was full of culture dishes;
beakers; dozens of flat bottles; a microscope; a homemade incu-
bator; a glassware sterilizer; a small centrifuge; and a good deal of
other equipment.*

*"What do you think it is, Lieutenant? Drugs? Crank?" Wash-
ington speculated, referring to the drug methamphetamine, which
is also known as "speed" on the street.*

*"Doesn't look like any crank factory I've ever seen," observed
Buel.*

*As the police officers examined the laboratory, Washington
stopped in front of a small walk-in storage closet. Inside, it appeared to be a cross between a pantry and a dark room. The only*

illumination was a dull red light. The shelves were stacked with dozens of thermos-like containers. Washington took one of the containers from the shelf and began to open it, but was interrupted by Buel.

"Don't touch anything," he ordered. "There's something strange about this place. I think we'd better get the Captain and some of the lab boys down here."

Washington returned the container to the shelf and the two men made a hasty exit from the laboratory. Buel posted Washington outside the door of the laboratory while he went upstairs to call for assistance.

Three hours later, Richmond's Chief of Police was buzzed by his secretary.

He stabbed at the intercom button on his phone and put the receiver to his ear.

"Yes?"

"It's Dr. Paschall."

"Talk fast, Ed," commanded the Chief when Paschall came on the line. "I've got to meet the press in less than ten minutes."

"You're not gonna like this one, Chief," began Paschall slowly. "The substance in those containers is Bacillus anthracis . . . *anthrax . . . millions of spores in dried form. Those crazies you shot it out with have stockpiled enough to wipe out half the state."*

Shock registered on the Chief's face. He slumped back in his chair and lit a cigarette. Muggers, rapists, burglars, murderers; he could deal with them all. But this was something else. Twenty-eight years of police work had not prepared him for what he had just heard.

"At least we got 'em before they could use the stuff," Dr. Paschall was saying.

"I-I'm not so sure about that, Ed," said the Chief. "We've got a report, confirmed by several of the neighbors, that a man was seen running from the rear of the house right after the shooting started, and he was carrying several silver containers that looked like thermos bottles."

"You mean we've got a looney on the loose with canisters of anthrax?"

"Looks that way, doesn't it?"

A Limitless Horizon of Targets

C/B weapons are highly versatile, capable of attacking almost an infinite range of targets, from whole nations to single individuals. An expertly executed attack could be carried out with little or no warning, causing thousands of casualties. In all likelihood, the perpetrators would escape and never be discovered.

The BDM study maintains that U.S. installations overseas are the most likely targets of a terrorist group armed with biological weapons, but it is hard to imagine attacks carried out within the borders of the United States. The threat is not new. In 1960, in a now famous statement, Major General Marshall Stubbs, head of the U.S. Army Chemical Corps, warned that an enemy armed with "dry biological material" could, with only ten aircraft, mount an attack against the United States that might kill or incapacitate 30 percent of the American people; that is, seventy million people. As recently as 1986, Soviet instructors at Cuban chemical warfare schools are reported to have said that Cuba had the capability to subject the United States to a similar level of contamination with toxins they have stockpiled.

Although an attack on a single building or facility, using the ventilation system to transmit the agent, remains the most likely scenario, nevertheless, a major attack on a U.S. city cannot be ruled out.

Terrorists, for example, might outfit an old tanker with internal tanks (suitable for the storage of a chemical or biological agent), powerful pressurized aerosol generators (which could turn the agent into a deadly cloud of vapor), and external booms. From all outward appearances it would look like just another rusting Liberian tanker as it passed through The Narrows heading toward New York. But off the tip of Manhattan it could crank up the generators and open the booms. Within minutes, if weather conditions were right, a great expanding cloud of lethal vapor would be drifting toward the World Trade Center towers. Because the vapor would likely be both odorless and colorless, and thus undetectable to any observer, the ship would be able to dock in New Jersey and the terrorists could escape before the authorities could pinpoint the source of the attack. If the attack was of biological character rather than chemical, it might take days or weeks for the effects to become evident, by which time the terrorists might be halfway around the world. Homes and buildings would provide little protection from the effects of the attack. A modern high-rise building with hermetically sealed windows would become a slaughterhouse as its ventilation systems sucked in the agent and circulated it throughout the building.

A major attack on a city could easily produce widespread panic and a general breakdown of societal order. Most of the population, even people in outlying areas, would flee as far and as fast as they could, creating monumental traffic jams. The evacuation would be anything but orderly. Fights, riots, and looting would occur. If an infectious biological agent were used by the terrorists, the panicking victims would spread the disease wherever they fled. In the aftermath of the attack, there likely would be a breakdown of communications, sanitation, food distribution, transport, and most important of all, medical care. Hospital facilities would be stretched to the limits, doctors would be in short supply, and burial facilities would be altogether inadequate for the task of disposing of bodies before the onset of additional health hazards. The United States has grown unprepared for almost any epidemic, a natural result of bringing such diseases under control. There is not even enough serum in the United States to protect five hundred people against anthrax.

A number of mock "attacks" on U.S. and Canadian cities and towns were conducted by the U.S. military during the 1950s using "harmless" bacteria. In one instance, two U.S. minesweepers, steaming in the waters just beyond Golden Gate Bridge, carried out six separate mock attacks on San Francisco, releasing sprays contaminated with *Bacillus globigii* and *Serratia marcescens*. Virtually all of the residents of San Francisco inhaled at least five thousand or more particles of the bacteria. Had this been a real attack, it would have been ample for most biological agents to cause infection. If the agent had been pneumonic plague, of those inhaling a thousand organisms or more, 75 percent would likely have developed the disease and required hospitalization. Eighty precent of those who had contracted the disease, if left untreated, would probably have died.

What makes plague such a frightening weapon is that once a

human chain of victims is started, the disease might continue to spread, unchecked, in secondary and tertiary outbreaks, for years to come, especially if an antibiotic-resistant strain were employed. The great plague that struck Europe in the fourteenth century produced a pandemic that wiped out nearly a quarter of the continent's population, or twenty-five million people, in five years.

Terrorists would not have to possess a large amount of any single agent. Random attacks with small C/B bombs scattered around a city, while not producing a large number of casualties, would almost assuredly create a major panic. One need only consider the fears generated by AIDS, throughout not only the general public but the medical community as well, to recognize the potential that a C/B weapon would have for creating terror. The detonation of five well-publicized C/B bombs would probably be enough to stampede the population of any city in the United States, turning even a megalopolis like New York into a virtual ghost town overnight.

In nations highly dependent on tourism, the contamination of a leading tourist hotel or national monument with a C/B weapon would all but ensure the ruin of the industry for many years. The initial association of AIDS with Haitians almost destroyed Haiti's tourist industry overnight. The psychological impact of an attack that contaminates a great national monument or landmark, and renders it dangerous to humans for weeks, months, or even years, is incalculable. Anthrax contamination of London's Hyde Park, Arlington National Cemetery, the Mayan ruins at Tikal in Guatemala, the grounds of the Palace of Versailles, or the Mall in Washington, D.C., would not present a particularly difficult challenge to terrorists, and would be front-page news around the world. Anthrax spores have been known to remain alive in the soil for decades, so returning such areas to active use would present a formidable (and expensive) challenge.

C/B weapons could be used to thwart U.S. policy aims around the globe. The day may not be far off when leftist terrorists in Central America, instead of waging a prolonged and costly guerrilla insurgency, might opt for a war in which deadly C/B agents are used to destabilize the target country and ultimately to bring down the government. C/B agents could be used to assassinate the nation's leadership, to poison foodstuffs and water supplies, and to attack the industrial sector, thus plunging the country into chaos. Defoliants and herbicides could be used to devastate crops, a particularly serious threat to monocultures. In many regions, the widespread destruction of plant life would be accompanied by serious, and often irreversible, soil erosion. Herbicides and defoliants could be used to poison irrigation ditches. If they were sprayed in pastures where dairy animals graze, would likely result in contaminated milk. The deliberate introduction of rice blast fungus in many parts of Asia could produce starvation and famine. Cereal rusts, rots, and mildews are difficult to control because no practical fungicides exist. Terrorists might even use arsenic to poison fishing areas, especially oyster and shrimp beds.

Attacks on livestock could be made with relative ease and virtually no immediately visible signature. Hogs can be infected with African swine fever or foot-and-mouth disease. Cattle are susceptible to Q fever, anthrax, Rift Valley fever, and foot-and-mouth disease. Chickens and turkeys have their own form of plague, and there are numerous diseases that attack sheep, goats, horses, and other livestock. Usually the only way of containing the disease is the mass slaughter of the infected animals, which could be a devastating economic blow to many poor countries.

In January 1984, an extortionist threatened to infect the livestock in Queensland state, Australia, with foot-and-mouth disease if certain prison reforms were not undertaken. Queensland is home to 60 percent of the Australian beef industry, so local authorities could not afford to take the threat lightly, and mobilized every available resource to track down the culprit. The Australian government even engaged in urgent and highly secret consultations with the United States and other allies. Ultimately the threat turned out to be a hoax perpetrated by a local convict, but the implications of such an attack were obvious, and Australian authorities concluded that it would be almost impossible to prevent one.

2
The Soviet Quest for
Ultimate Weapons

Motivation and Baseline Plans

Classified data on Soviet military programs are scarce in the West. The rare glimpses we obtain are almost always the result of human intelligence, or HUMINT, as it is called in intelligence circles. The best HUMINT comes from spies and defectors. But the "best" is not without its problems, the chief of which is how to evaluate the source. Is the source good, or are we deliberately being fed a mixture of good and bad information by a double agent? This problem was made embarrassingly clear in the summer and fall of 1984 when a KGB officer, Colonel Vitaly Yurchenko, defected to the United States. Yurchenko was widely heralded as a source of great value. A high CIA official who was formerly in charge of clandestine operations even stated that he would stake his career on Yurchenko's bona fides, roughly forty-eight hours before Yurchenko redefected to the Soviet Union. Yurchenko's flight instantly brought his testimony into question, and, along with it, that of several other recent defectors.

One defector's testimony has been proven correct and of great value over the years: that of the Czechoslovak political officer, General Major Jan Sejna. Sejna is even more noteworthy because he is also the highest ranking official in the actual decision-making process to have defected from the East. Sejna was the first person to provide detailed information regarding Soviet involvement in international terrorism; on the detailed functioning of the all-important

Defense Council; on Soviet long-range plans for the world revolutionary movement; on Soviet operational plans for the invasion of Austria and Switzerland in the event of war; on turning Cuba into a Soviet revolutionary center; and on numerous Warsaw Pact infiltration, subversion, and disinformation operations.

Sejna came to the West in 1968 with a treasure trove of information that he had accumulated from the numerous high-level offices he had held prior to his defection. He had been a member of the Central Committee of the Communist Party of Czechoslovakia, the National Assembly, the Main Political Administration, the Administration Department, and the Ministry of Defense. He was on the Presidium at the National Assembly and the Bureau of the Main Political Administration. At the Ministry of Defense he was first secretary, chief of cabinet, member of the Kolegium, and head of the Main Party Group. But most importantly, he was the secretary of the Czechoslovak Defense Council, whose counterpart, the Soviet Defense Council, is the highest decision-making body in the communist system, with authority over defense, national security, foreign policy, intelligence and counterintelligence, and major influence over finance, R&D and industry. His testimony on Soviet interests and activities pertaining to C/B warfare is both sobering and disquieting. Most importantly, it provides the essential foundation for interpreting other intelligence, including the testimony of numerous Soviet émigrés. His story is worth repeating in detail.

Sejna begins his story by pointing out that during the 1950s, the highest priority in the Soviet Union was the development of nuclear weapons and strategy. Bringing the Soviet Union into the nuclear age was the preeminent goal for planning, training, education, and industrial expansion. However, though C/B weapons, along with many other categories of weapons, took a back seat to the nuclear programs, they were not out of mind. Indeed, unlike the West, the Soviets have never regarded nuclear weapons as absolute weapons. All weapons and forces are considered important, even in nuclear war, and this dictum applied with special distinction to C/B weapons.

In the 1950s the Soviets recognized that chemical weapons were, in many respects, comparable to nuclear weapons; hence, they labeled both "weapons of mass destruction" and considered chemical weapons as equivalents or substitutes for nuclear weapons, at least for those of lower yields. They also recognized that such weapons were regarded with extreme distaste in the West; so much so that they believed this was one area where the West could be made to unilaterally disarm. To accomplish this, the Soviets believed it was necessary that they be viewed in the West as in full compliance with the 1925 Geneva Protocol against C/B warfare. Hence, all offensive C/B weapons programs were placed under a cloak of extreme secrecy. Where is was necessary to refer to such Soviet munitions or programs, they were called "special weapons" or sometimes "nuclear type 2 weapons." In operations plans and exercises, special code words, such as BUTTERFLY and SPRUCE, were used to refer to C/B weapons.

By 1960, the Soviet nuclear weapons development program was well under way, and C/B weapons development quickly emerged as a high-priority activity throughout the Warsaw Pact. The first indication of this growth was the promulgation of new intelligence initiatives in 1961. All Warsaw Pact countries were directed to increase their technical espionage. At the top of the priority list was C/B research in the West. Soon thereafter, special new facilities for the development of C/B weapons were built. Czechoslovakia, which was one of the lead satellite countries in technical matters, was assigned an important role in both chemical and biological weapons development. In 1962, Czechoslovakia built a new institute for the development of biological weapons.

Within three years, the Soviet C/B weapons programs were in high gear. The rationale for the high priority accorded these weapons was explained in a lecture by Soviet Marshal A.I. Antonov, the chief of staff of the Warsaw Pact forces. In the long term, he reportedly explained, it was possible that the use of nuclear weapons might be prohibited. As a result, C/B weapons would become weapons of decisive importance. The improvement of chemical weapons and the development of "super" biological weapons, therefore, was a vital task.

Moreover, in assessing the various enemies of the Warsaw Pact, Antonov pointed out that the People's Republic of China (PRC) represented a special problem, because it was relatively immune to nuclear weapons owing to its great territory and massive population.

The only way to deal with the PRC was with C/B weapons. This conclusion was repeated shortly thereafter by Marshal Andrei Grechko in a private conversation. He added that the only one way to fight the Chinese was "to make them sleep forever."

Sejna was party to a second significant conversation—a 1963 Moscow discussion between General Secretary Nikita S. Khrushchev and Marshal Rodion Malinovsky. Malinovsky had just asserted, "Comrade Khrushchev, I believe socialism will be established and remain wherever Soviet tanks are present." Khrushchev thoughtfully countered, "Rodion Yakovlezich, between you and me there is a big difference. You would like to see Soviet tanks everywhere today. For me, tomorrow is sufficient. I don't want to burn Europe; I want German industry intact to build socialism."

Since 1963, the use of C/B weapons has been regarded as the best way to seize Europe without destroying it in the event of war. The war could not be won by obliterating the territory. Soldiers would have to be able to enter and occupy Western Europe. This was perceived as the essential condition for victory. The large-scale use of nuclear weapons would be counterproductive because they would destroy the prize and threaten troop operations. Accordingly, C/B weapons took on a new and dominant role. They would be used to create chaos in NATO's rear, prevent mobilization, paralyze political–administration centers, and disrupt force readiness. In the aftermath, conventional forces would deliver the coup de grace.

These words were backed up with a wide variety of actions in Czechoslovakia and throughout the Warsaw Pact, most of which began in 1963 or shortly thereafter. War plans began to incorporate the assumption that C/B weapons would be used. Division commanders were given authority to employ chemical weapons in the event of war. On the other hand, biological weapons were considered strategic, with decision authority for their use held by the supreme commander of Warsaw Pact forces. Military training was revised to intensify the training for crossing contaminated areas. Also beginning in 1963, the Soviets directed that henceforth all war materiel projects had to incorporate chemical and biological warfare (CBW) protection, and all presentations on new military equipment to the Defense Council had to show how the improvements were designed to provide CBW protection.

In Czechoslovakia, as in the Soviet Union, the major portion of C/B weapons research was funded through and managed by the Czechoslovak Academy of Sciences in response to orders emanating from the operational plan of the General Staff. The head of Czechoslovak research and development was academician Dr. Ivan Malek, a highly respected biological scientist. At that time, Czechoslovakia was a world leader in microbiology, and Malek ranked among the world's top scientists. Malek was openly listed as the director of the Czechoslovak Biological Institute. He was also a member of the National Assembly vice chairman of the Czechoslovak Academy of Sciences. In secret, he was the director of the main military biological warfare institute. (Malek's positions are roughly comparable to those held by the Soviet academician believed to be in charge of USSR biological warfare research today.) Malek's wife, as Sejna recalled, was a doctor who worked at the main military hospital in Prague, running biological warfare experiments.

In 1964, plans were laid for the deployment of chemical munitions in Czechoslovakia. In 1965, the special importance of research was officially described in a secret speech by the head of the Science Administration at the Czechoslovak Ministry of Defense. This administration had been set up to integrate science and technical development, and to ensure a more orderly and speedy transition of scientific developments into military hardware. The director's speech, "On the Problems of Military Politics of the Czechoslovak Communist Party in the Light of the Thirteenth Party Congress," had its origins in secret directives from the Soviet Union. It presaged the beginning of joint teams and new institutes. In a paragraph focusing on new weapons developments that would *not* be of "a merely evolutionary character," the director presented four examples: means for a reliable antimissile and antispace defense; warfare in space; military applicability of quantum generators; and C/B warfare, where "new developments during the next 10–15 years may bring about further decisive changes in the development and military applicability of chemical and biological weapons."

One of the programs that the Czechoslovak scientists were working on under direct Soviet supervision (because of its sensitivity) was the delivery of biological weapons from space. The Soviets had classified this program above the "top-secret" level (specifically,

it was classified "state importance") because it was in direct violation of the UN resolution against the militarization of space.

Later the same year, a long-term, twenty-year plan for the development of C/B weapons was completed and coordinated with
the Soviet plan. Phase one (1965–71) emphasized qualitative steps;
research; preparation for new weapons production; and preparation and protection of troops. This plan placed unusually heavy emphasis on research to develop new weapons. For example, 15 percent of PVO (air defense) cadres were assigned to R&D. In the case
of chemical cadres, 35 percent were assigned to chemical warfare
research; the biological warfare percentage was still higher.

This plan also stressed intelligence (espionage) and deception.
In the latter case, Sejna explained, the Vietnam War provided "fantastic cover." Vietnam was the focus of attention. Soviet propaganda helped create this situation, especially regarding the publicity
associated with the U.S. use of defoliants such as Agent Orange.
This publicity was used to deflect attention from the Warsaw Pact
activities, especially those in C/B warfare.

In reviewing the emergence of C/B warfare in Soviet and Warsaw Pact strategy, Sejna views 1967 as the watershed year. The previous year, the massive use of C/B weapons had been "tested" for
the first time in a major Warsaw Pact exercise, Voltava. The Soviets
had decided in 1966 to use C/B weapons in Third World countries
rather than nuclear weapons, even in those countries that were U.S.
allies or had allowed the United States to have military bases. This
use of nonnuclear weapons of mass destruction against the West
and its allies was tested in a Middle East scenario exercise in 1967,
coincident, as it turned out, with the Six-Day War. Indeed, by 1967,
there was considerable evidence that the twenty-year plan initiated
in 1965 was well on its way to being implemented.

Most importantly, the massive use of C/B weapons was formally
incorporated into all Warsaw Pact operational plans in 1967. At
this time, chemical weapons were envisioned for use mainly in combat areas against military and military–industrial targets. Authority
for their use was held at division level. In contrast, biological weapons, whose use required the approval of the Warsaw Pact com-
mander-in-chief, were designed to be employed in noncombat areas,
specifically (1) to paralyze whole regions and even countries,

thereby preventing them from joining the war; (2) to poison areas where enemy airborne forces might land: (3) to liquidate the bureaucratic and political elite of capitalist nations; (4) to destroy the masses of the People's Republic of China; and (5) as sabotage agents for use by *spetsnaz* (KGB) and diversionary (GRU) units. Wherever possible, the use of biological agents was to be accompanied by a disinformation and deception campaign designed to shift the blame to NATO.

The Soviets also brought their Eastern bloc satellites into their long-range planning process in 1967. The primary guiding document, "The Long-Range Plan for the Next Ten to Fifteen Years and Beyond," was distributed to each country to use in preparing coordinated long-range plans for defeat of the West. In that document, C/B weapons were given prominent attention. Specifically, the goal was set for the introduction of an entirely new, qualitatively different family of C/B weapons by 1985.

Thus, the 1960s ended with the Soviets embarked on an aggressive program of C/B weapons development. Their objective was to make C/B weapons even more effective than nuclear weapons, so effective that they might one day be substituted for nuclear weapons in Soviet plans.

The Soviets had such a high regard for the potential of C/B weapons that they undertook two parallel programs. The first program, focusing on the near term, was to incorporate what might be called more traditional C/B weapons (representing technology of the 1960s) into Warsaw Pact forces and plans. Preparation for producing and employing the latest versions of these weapons and preparing Warsaw Pact forces for operating in contaminated areas had begun in 1965. All Warsaw Pact forces were to be fully prepared and equipped by 1976.

The second program focused on the long term, and was to develop an entirely new family of capabilities based on the latest technology: biotechnology and genetic engineering. The second program began with research in the mid 1960s. The nature of the concepts embraced and techniques employed are evident from the Soviet and Eastern European C/B weapons literature during the period of 1968–71. This is when neurotoxins, psychotoxins, small-molecular-weight proteins, and synthetic peptides, "the most malefic development in military toxicology," were discussed as the C/B weapons of the future. This is also precisely the time when the United States closed its eyes to the Soviet activities and to the potential of the new technology.

Scenario Five: The Reefs off the Isle of Youth, Cuba

At first the Cuban government did not know what to make of them. First dozens, then hundreds, of their troops in Angola and other parts of West Africa were struck down with a strange malady that undermined the body's natural ability to resist disease and infection and that was transmitted chiefly through sexual intercourse. Eastern European specialists brought in to treat those afflicted finally threw up their hands in frustration and admitted defeat, advising the Cubans as they felt that a "cure" was beyond the reach of medical science at the present time.

Authorities were concerned over the possible spread of the disease to the Cuban population at large. They worried that public knowledge regarding the risk of contracting the disease would promote discord in the ranks and increase the growing resistance to Castro's African adventurism within the military. Thus, the Cuban government sought to isolate those with the disease, warehousing them in remote military camps and hospitals designated as psychiatric care centers, and suppressed any information about the disease itself. As Cuban veterans already absorbed back into society were diagnosed as suffering from the illness, they were discharged from their jobs and provided with outpatient care at special clinics. Without employment and forced to subsist on a minimal stipend, those suffering from the disease became outcasts, a new class of "untouchables," and gradually they fell into crime, prostitution, and various forms of antisocial behavior. It was not long before Cuba's prison population contained a large percentage of diseased inmates, given the close confinement and the rampant homosexuality that characterizes men in captivity.

Frequently, leaky Haitian boats full of economic refugees heading for the United States washed up on Cuban shores or were inter-

dicted in Cuban waters, and the hapless people aboard were tossed into Cuban prisons for a few days, sometimes weeks, before being shipped back to Haiti. While in prison, even if only briefly, a number of Haitians contracted the cruel disease. Once back in Port-au-Prince, the former boat people were ostracized by the Haitian government for their effrontery in trying to leave for a better life; they were prevented from normal work or status. Many found work in the thriving homosexual bars and brothels that the government tolerated as a method of obtaining desperately needed foreign exchange. Publications targeted at gay audiences in Europe and the United States even printed pictures of young boys (available for what amounted to a pittance) to lure homosexual travelers to Haiti. Haiti quickly became a homosexual mecca, whose delights were passed along by word of mouth throughout San Francisco's Castro Street neighborhood, around Washington's Dupont Circle, and up and down the beaches of New York's Fire Island.

Gay vacationers returning home (surfeited with Haitian sun and sex) did not know that many of them had become carriers of the killer virus that attacked the body's immune system, and that some of them would soon contract the disease and transmit it to others.

Meanwhile, by 1980 pressures were building in Cuba for the exodus of thousands of Cubans intent on seeking freedom in the United States. Following incidents at several foreign legations, Castro opened the doors to all Cubans who wanted to leave via the port of Mariel. In response, hundreds of small boats set out from Florida to collect family members and other refugees and bring them to Miami. The Mariel boatlift had begun.

On the converted Soviet minesweeper that served as his personal yacht, a dripping Fidel Castro had just shed his scuba gear and walked over to one of the ammunition lockers, which was loaded with cold beer on ice. He scooped up a Miller, popped the tab, and guzzled the cold liquid, leaving a ring of foam on his beard and moustache. He wiped the foam away with the back of his hand and settled into one of the deck chairs to finish the last chapter of a science fiction novel he had begun the previous day.

He hadn't finished more than a page when one of the crewmen interrupted him, pointing out the approach of a fast launch bearing the ensign of his brother, Raúl, operational chief of Cuba's armed *forces and number-two man in the government. The smaller vessel dropped anchor alongside, and Raúl, followed by two East German bodyguards, scaled the rope ladder to the deck of the minesweeper. Tall, frowning, dressed in full camouflage gear, he gave his brother a perfunctory "abrazo" and then took a seat across from him, the East German guards at his back.*

After a few pleasantries were exchanged, Raúl came directly to the point.

"Fidel, it was a brilliant decision to permit the miscreants in our society, those indifferent to building a worker's paradise, to leave. I say good riddance to them all." He turned northward and flicked his upper teeth with this thumbnail in an obscene gesture of disdain.

Fidel accepted the compliment with a nod and then motioned to a steward to bring him another beer. He invited Raúl to join him, but his brother begged off. Raúl, he knew, was a solitary drinker, not a gregarious one, but he always offered nonetheless.

"Now, Fidel. I have an idea, and that is what brings me out to see you today." Raúl waited for Fidel to open the beer and get settled again so that none of his words would be missed. "I've been thinking, why don't we send the Yankees the scum of our jails and mental wards? Let the United States support them. Needless to say, it will save us millions of pesos and relieve us of a great headache. What do you say, Fidel?"

Fidel pulled a long corona from a box on the deck next to his chair and rolled it around in his mouth thoughtfully. "I like it, Raúl," said Fidel with a smile. "I like it. Give the order." He laughed aloud and gestured expressively with his cigar. "I wish I could see the look on Jimmy Carter's face when he sees what we've sent him."

Raúl rose slowly to his feet. "One other thing, Fidel. What about those with the disease," he said in hushed terms, "the ones whose immune systems have broken down? Why don't we get rid of them too? We can force the boats at Mariel to take them along with the others."

Fidel thought about it for a moment. "Like a form of biological warfare, eh?"

"Exactly," agreed Raúl. "Just as we undermine Yankee society by encouraging the flow of drugs into Florida and by training terrorists and sowing unrest among the Puerto Ricans, so we could

*seed their people with this disease. It would be like a time bomb."
His eyes narrowed to slits. "Perhaps even more important," he
chuckled, "our problem becomes their problem, eh?"*

*"Hey, that's good," laughed Fidel. "The way I see it, we win
both ways: not only does it disrupt Yankee society, but with all of
their doctors and hospitals, if they find a cure for it, they will have
to share it with us. Medicine knows no politics, and all that."*

*Both men laughed heartily as they rose to their feet. Fidel
draped his arm around Raúl and walked him across the deck to the
rope ladder.*

*"I'm glad you're on our side," Fidel called after Raúl as his
launch began to sputter away.*

Soviet Buildup, American Indifference

Next to World War I, when the mass use of chemical warfare agents
was first witnessed, the decade of the seventies was the most event-
ful time span in the history of C/B warfare. This was the decade
when advances in the chemical and biological sciences revolutionized the broad field of life sciences.

The potentials of the scientific developments about to unfold
were clear at the start of the decade, both in the United States and
in the Soviet Union. Thus, in 1970, U.S. Nobel laureate Joshua
Lederberg warned that recent advances in molecular biology "might
be exploited for military purposes and result in a biological weapons race whose aim could well become the most efficient means for
removing man from the planet." He further argued that through
genetic and chemical manipulation, "the potential undoubtedly exists for the design and development of infective agents against
which no credible defense is possible." Even more sinister possibilities were discussed by Eastern European scientists at a symposium
in East Berlin the following year. In addition to superinfective
agents, they spoke of toxins and new substances that could "cause
psychic disturbances when present even in minute quantities in the
air," of "substances that render people incapable of fighting," and
of psychotoxins directed "against the further existence of an inde-

pendently thinking and acting society." By the end of the decade, there was no questioning the credibility of the scientists' estimates or the myriad of other possibilities that had arisen.

It is difficult to conceive of a less propitious time for the United States to leave the field of C/B warfare, but this is exactly what happened. In December 1969 President Nixon renounced biological warfare and stated that the United States would unilaterally destroy its stocks of such weapons. Early the following year the president extended this decision to include toxins.

The story behind these White House decisions is a story of intrigue involving double agents and successful Soviet deception. At the time, the FBI had been operating a clandestine source inside the Soviet government, code-named "Fedora." Fedora's bona fides had been considered good, but intelligence officials now reluctantly admit that he was a double agent working for the KGB. In 1969, Fedora was used by the Soviets to send a false message to President Nixon. The essence of this message was that the Soviets were concerned over the massive U.S. chemical warfare (CW) and biological warfare (BW) capabilities in comparison to a backward and inferior Soviet capability. The Soviets wanted the White House to believe that the USSR had decided to redress this imbalance unless some other answer could be found. They did not want to begin a C/B arms race, according to Fedora, because of the many other pressing demands on their economy. They wished there was a way both sides could exert restraint.

This same message also was conveyed via other means. The desired response, for the United States to move out of the C/B weapons field, was further encouraged by the massive anti-U.S. propaganda associated with the U.S. use of the defoliant Agent Orange in Vietnam, and by the anti–chemical warfare propaganda following the mass poisoning of several thousand sheep near Dugway Proving Grounds in Utah, which was falsely blamed on faulty open air testing of nerve agent.

When the secret Soviet "offer" was received, the White House was quick to take action. Following a rushed pro forma analysis of the chemical warfare situation by the policy experts in the Defense Department, who "voted against" the action, President Nixon renounced biological and toxin warfare, presumably accepting the Soviet offer. In the years that followed, the United States rapidly went out of the C/B warfare business. The United States signed the Biological and Toxin Weapons convention in 1972 (which the Senate ratified), and signed the 1925 Geneva Protocol against the use of asphyxiating gas three years later. The U.S. Army shut down its chemical warfare school and even decided to disband its Chemical Corps in 1974. The United States continued to possess the chemical weapons manufactured in the 1960s, but for all practical purposes, there was no offensive or defensive C/B warfare capability by the mid-1970s. In the name of détente and arms control, the United States' C/B warfare capability had been all but wiped out.

Meanwhile, the Soviet buildup progressed in an inexorable manner. By 1975 U.S. intelligence had clear indications of Soviet capabilities and intent. Training of troops in contaminated environments had increased enormously, and the status of the chemical troops had been upgraded. Beginning in late 1973, the United States began to analyze Soviet equipment that had been captured by the Israelis in the Yom Kippur War. The analyses showed that all the vehicles were CW and BW protected. Additionally, captured CW antidote kits and BW sensors and diagnostic equipment were found to be far better than even the counterpart U.S. equipment still in development.

On the biological side, new construction and expansion had been identified at five biological warfare facilities; a special division within the Soviet microbiology industry had been created for the express purpose of developing new biological weapons; and Soviets who attended a special scientific conference that was convened in 1975 to discuss potential problems in gene-splicing research caused several U.S. scientists to become concerned that the real Soviet interest was not scientific, but rather related to biological warfare.

The data on the methodical expansion of Soviet biological warfare activity were sufficiently alarming that officials with the Arms Control and Disarmament Agency (ACDA) notified the White House about the possible violations. However, no action was taken. The intelligence was dismissed ostensibly because administration officials found it unlikely that "the Soviets would derive any significant benefit in circumventing the terms of the convention, and there is no convincing evidence that contradicts the Soviet public statement that they have been in full compliance with the convention." The real reason, of course, was political, and represented the triumph of hope over hard evidence as the administration sought vainly to fan the flickering embers of détente.

Nothing was to change the U.S. attitude until 1979, when an accident occurred at the Soviet biological warfare facility, Cantonment 19, in Sverdlovsk. An explosion resulted in the release of a large cloud of pulmonary anthrax bacilli, or possibly anthrax spores, that drifted over the adjacent area and out into the surrounding countryside. The Soviet military quickly established control over the whole region; restricted travel in or out of the area; vaccinated people; placed the sick in specially guarded hospitals; sprayed the area with the decontaminant chloramine; and sealed all dead bodies in special coffins. The number of people that died in the two weeks immediately following the incident is believed by U.S. officials to be between two hundred and a thousand. Though this event, coupled with the other equally damning evidence, finally caused the U.S. intelligence community to acknowledge that the Soviets were still in business of biological warfare—and in a big way— it had little impact on U.S. defense thinking. Nor has it resulted in any noteworthy U.S. response.

At almost the same time as the Sverdlovsk accident, a handful of U.S. officials became interested in reports and data that had been emanating from Southeast Asia for four years on the occurrence of strange rain, predominately yellow in color, that was being used by Soviet and Vietnamese military forces against the hill tribes and "rebels" in Vietnam, Laos, and Kampuchea. The chemicals were causing ghastly medical problems, and death, among the inhabitants of remote villages. Shortly after the Soviets invaded Afghanistan in December 1979, similar incidents were reported by Afghan refugees fleeing the country, and by medical personnel who were assisting with the evacuation.

Fortuitously, a key civilian in the army medical intelligence laboratory, Dr. Sharon Watson (who had recently completed her doctoral work in the area of mycotoxins), recognized certain telltale attributes in the data and ordered detailed chemical tests for the presence of mycotoxins. The tests were positive. Subsequent data, including the testing of residue on captured Soviet gasmasks, confirmed the initial findings. Despite the numerous critics, who initially challenged the data and results, the inevitable conclusions are generally accepted by qualified observers. It is clear that the Soviets were using lethal toxic agents, both chemicals and toxins, in the conflicts in Afghanistan and Southeast Asia, and were providing the lethal toxic material, training, and other assistance to their various surrogate forces, all of which is disallowed under the 1972 Convention and the 1925 Geneva Protocol.

In September 1981 the new Secretary of State, Alexander Haig, startled the world with his announcement from West Berlin that the United States had determined that the Soviets were using toxins, specifically mycotoxins, in violation of the 1972 Biological and Toxin Weapons Convention. He did not need to mention that the mycotoxins were only one of several prohibited agents being employed, nor that the Soviets appeared to be experimenting with new and quite unusual agents.

This announcement was the first event to generate some type of a U.S. response. In a sense, it was a vindication for the relative handful of U.S. defense and military officials who, since intelligence on growing Soviet chemical warfare capabilities and related U.S. vulnerabilities had become available in 1974, had been pushing hard to awaken the military establishment to the need for increased chemical warfare defense preparations. For the most part, their efforts went unheeded until Secretary Haig's announcement focused new attention on the whole issue of C/B defense preparations. Almost immediately, both the budget for chemical defense and efforts to introduce a new family of munitions into the U.S. defense arsenal—so-called binary munitions—began to increase substantially. Reluctantly, the Defense Department began to acknowledge what the Soviets had set in motion in 1965: the mass use of chemicals in a European battlefield context. Unfortunately, the battle to achieve even this modest and tardy (by fifteen years) response has been difficult and time-consuming. During this process, the national security community has been distracted from the more dangerous threat posed by new technology, the most dangerous and far-reaching elements of which the Soviets initiated in 1965.

Perhaps the first real glimpse of this threat surfaced in the testimony of Soviet émigré Mark Popovskiy, who appeared before the House Permanent Select Committee on Intelligence on 29 May 1980. He reported on his numerous conversations with Soviet scientists on biological warfare programs. Popovskiy had been called to testify on the anthrax accident at the Soviet military biological warfare facility at Sverdlovsk. He elaborated on the evidence of Soviet work in C/B warfare (including their practice of conducting tests on human guinea pigs). Almost as an afterthought Popovskiy recalled a 1975 meeting at which Dr. Yuri A. Ovchinnikov, a high official at the USSR Academy of Sciences, had explained to a group of young talented scientists that it was necessary to use genetic engineering to create bacteriological weapons. Ovchinnikov was clearly not referring to defensive applications. "If we bring the Central Committee of the Communist Party of the Soviet Union vaccines, nobody will pay attention to it," Ovchinnikov was quoted as saying, "but if we bring a virus, oh, then this will be recognized by all as a great victory."

Dr. Ovchinnikov has now been identified as the scientific father of the modern Soviet biochem warfare effort. He earned his doctorate in biochemistry in 1966. Four years later he was appointed director of the Institute of Bioorganic Chemistry and academician of the Academy of Sciences. In 1974, at age 39, he was promoted to vice president of the academy. He was subsequently awarded several prizes, including the Lenin Prize and Hero of Socialist Labor, and was made a candidate member of the Central Committee in 1981. Overall, this is a good indication of the importance and recognition accorded his work by the party. All his fields of technical expertise have direct relevance to C/B warfare: bioregulation; ion transport through membranes; and peptides and peptide synthesis. In a sense, his career bears an interesting resemblance to the Czechoslovak Academician Malek, who headed the Czechoslovak biological warfare program in the 1960s.

Even Popovskiy's 1980 remarks about the Soviet scientist Ovchinnikov and the Soviet program to apply the fruits of genetic engineering to biological warfare drew little attention in the press. They were accorded only passing interest by defense planners and analysts. National security attention in the United States remained focused on the traditional chemical warfare threat.

The pivotal change in perceptions occurred in the summer of 1983 with the testimony of a second Russian émigré whose report strengthened and significantly expanded the testimony of Mark Popovskiy. In response, intelligence efforts were improved to better understand both the traditional chemical warfare threat and the hazards posed by new technology.

The potential threat posed by the Soviet chemical warfare program and the USSR's emphasis on new technology began to appear in the press in the United States during this same period. Slowly the facts began to emerge in a series of official documents made public, unofficial leaks, and investigative reporting. One of the first important public disclosures appeared in a Jack Anderson report. The topics of the report were a new top-secret CIA assessment, and an associated summary notice to the president, warning him of newly discovered Soviet efforts in biotech warfare employing gene-splicing techniques to produce "super-viruses more deadly than any known to man today." Two months later, in April 1983, the Defense Department, in its third edition of *Soviet Military Power,* added a section on "Soviet Biological Warfare," in which they stated that there was "an apparent effort on the part of the Soviets to transfer selected aspects of genetic engineering research to their biological warfare centers."

In April, the *Wall Street Journal* began publishing a series entitled "Beyond 'Yellow Rain'" by William Kucewicz. The first episode was the "Soviets Search for Eerie New Weapons." Over the following five weeks, Kucewicz described the results of nearly nine months' research, based in part on extensive interviews with numerous scientist émigrés from the Soviet Union. He examined the people, technologies, research institutes, and the literature involved, and concluded with a discussion of the reasons that arms control had failed.

In his series, Kucewicz warned that there was an extensive high-priority program in the Soviet Union charged with applying genetic engineering to biological warfare. He described the program administered by the USSR Academy of Sciences and directed by Ovchinnikov, involving numerous laboratories throughout the Soviet Union and Eastern Europe. According to Kucewicz, though the program is protected by a heavy veil of secrecy, over two dozen émigrés have provided convincing evidence that it exists. One émigré confided to Kucewicz that he believed a group of Soviet scientists was engaged in an effort to splice toxin-producing genes into the DNA of a common flu virus. Other credible reports that reached the West concerned Soviet interest in neurotoxins for military and intelligence applications. The "Beyond Yellow Rain" series generated scattered criticism, but by far the dominant reaction was one of silence—a silence almost as eerie as the new weapons themselves.

The lack of any significant reaction to the new information is puzzling, especially when viewed in light of the information's tremendous scientific potential and the obvious military, political, and intelligence implications. There has been ample warning of the dire consequences flowing from inaction in face of the overwhelming and growing Soviet C/B threat. Each time new revelations are disclosed, there appears to be consensus in policy-making circles that something must be done, but this is where the reaction stops.

At present the United States appears to be caught in a catch-22 situation. More information is urgently needed. But the intelligence community rightly questions focusing more effort and attention on the area because there is no customer. The military is one obvious customer, but it generally does not like C/B weapons. Moreover, they know full well that should they devote substantial time and resources to the problem, not to mention the prestige of the uniformed services, it will only produce heated controversy and call into question many of their existing strategies, doctrines, and material acquisition programs. Accordingly they exhibit little more than token interest, and actively avoid the subject. As stated by the chief of army chemical planning, in referring to a comprehensive medical intelligence agency briefing on the Soviet activities, "Don't pay any attention to that, it's only a fourth-rate briefing."

These attitudes will have to change soon, lest the United States run a grave and terrible risk to its national security. It is no longer possible to ignore the inevitable. The possibilities of the new technology are too evident and too frightening to be ignored indefinitely. The applications are too deadly.

Scenario Six: Northern Nicaragua

Fighting cocks, like miniature gladiators, strutted about the grounds of the isolated hacienda, their razor-sharp spurs covered with tiny leather sheaths to prevent the valuable birds from tearing one another apart. The surrounding cane fields buzzed with insects in the sweltering heat of the afternoon. From the dark fringes of the nearby jungle (which provided a leafy refuge to everything that crept, crawled, or slithered) came shriek-like bird calls and the cries of howler monkeys. In the humid recesses of the jungle were rivers full of leeches, mosquitos as big as dragonflies, lizards, snakes of every imaginable variety, and spiders the size of a man's fist. Although the edge of the jungle was at least one-half mile distant, the odor of the jungle hung over the hacienda—the foul stench of rotting vegetation and stagnant water.

As two men and a woman, wearing heavy backpacks and carrying spraying equipment, strode toward a small outbuilding some distance from the main house, a faint but spreading rumble of thunder—a prelude to the afternoon deluge—drifted over the scene. Swollen rain clouds swirled overhead. A guard in camouflage fatigues, clutching a Czech-made VZ58V assault rifle, standing outside the door under a small porch, straightened to attention as the three figures passed by.

It was dim inside the little hut; a single twenty-five-watt bulb hanging from the ceiling burned weakly, throwing off a small circle of sickly light. The windows were covered over with thick burlap. Strips of plaster hung from the sweating walls, and the air was close and humid.

They stripped off the backpacks and equipment under the watchful gaze of a fat, bearded, sweat-soaked man, a cigar stuck in the corner of his mouth, who sat on a rickety chair behind a small table littered with Spanish-language comic books. He wore jump boots, baggy fatigue pants, and a gray shirt full of holes.

"How'd it go, Captain Bravo?" he asked disinterestedly, as they

hid the backpacks and equipment beneath a pile of crates and feed sacks.

"No problems," answered Captain Bravo, a thick-featured Latin with dark glasses, beret, and Disney World tee-shirt. "We sprayed the banana plantation exactly like they said. No one interfered with us. Tomorrow we hit another one."

"It is crazy, if you ask me," observed the fat sergeant, lifting his ponderous bulk from the chair with effort. "Risking our lives to make war on bananas. Have the comandantes in Managua gone soft in the brain?"

"Quiet!" commanded Captain Bravo. "That is why you are merely a sergeant and they are comandantes. Because you don't think." He tapped the side of his head. "So long as the Yankee stooges in Honduras permit their territory to be used by the Contras, we will never defeat them. They can always elude our grasp, just as we were able to escape the dictator Somoza's reach by slipping over the border into Costa Rica. In Honduras the Contras can lick their wounds and regroup to hit us again. Honduras is the key, but it is not without vulnerabilities. The banana is everything to that country; the chief export and the source of its foreign exchange. By infecting their bananas with canker, we undermine the economy and, as conditions decline, unrest will build. The Yankees will be forced to pour even more money into Tegucigalpa to keep the country afloat, to keep their puppets in power and to keep the lid on the situation as the frustration of the people mounts. We accomplish more in this way than we do by wiping out a whole Contra brigade. Much more. Now do you see?"

The sergeant hung his head and picked a flake of tobacco off his tongue. "If you say so Captain; but it still seems silly to me. We joined the Nacionales to make war on the colonialists and exploiters, not on bananas."

The Biotechnology Revolution

In the mid-1970s, major advances in molecular biology triggered a scientific revolution that almost instantly encompassed all the life sciences. During the years that followed, our knowledge of cellular processes, genetics, immunology, bioregulation, and neurochemistry, to mention but a few of the many affected disciplines, advanced more than it had in the previous hundred years. In this same short span of time, machines that could synthesize small-molecular-weight proteins were developed; the first artificial human hormone was produced and marketed; data banks of genes were assembled; and the isolation and manufacture of antibodies to attack a wide variety of diseases commenced.

This revolution in the life sciences has become known as the biotechnology revolution. Its central ingredient is genetic engineering. The revolution is noteworthy not only because of its impact on our understanding of the molecular basis of the life processes, but because of the almost instantaneous commercialization of the knowledge. The revolution is not confined to the laboratory. New genetic engineering firms emerged as the hottest stocks on Wall Street in the early 1980s. Every industrialized nation now has major national research programs under way in this area. The potential benefits are enormous and universally recognized.

Unfortunately, the downside risk—the potential for evil—is equally great. It is now possible to design diseases that are resistant to all known treatments. It is also possible to create artificial toxic proteins that can interfere with the immune system or with the bioregulation process. As knowledge is acquired to enable mental disorders to be more successfully treated, it will also be possible to induce these same disorders in human beings. And organisms formerly friendly to the human body can be turned into miniature production plants able to manufacture the most toxic substances, and even to do so on command. All this is possible today, and yet the revolution is only just beginning. The best and the worst lie ahead.

In the mid-1970s, two developments played a major role in triggering the revolution: recombinant DNA (rDNA) and monoclonal antibodies (MCA). The genetic material of a cell is a very large molecule composed of DNA. DNA acts as a blueprint for making the chemicals (proteins) needed for various cellular processes. The specific segment of DNA that encodes a particular protein is called a gene. In rDNA, which was first successfully performed in 1973, a gene from one cell's DNA is extracted and inserted into the DNA of another cell(the host DNA). If the conditions are proper, the original gene will continue to encode the particular protein in the host cell.

Certain genes of plants, fish, reptiles, and bacteria produce proteins that are highly poisonous toxins and can cause sickness—often death—if they come in contact with or are ingested by humans. The most potent of these toxins are often scarce and hard to obtain. They are not viable C/B warfare agents because they are not presently available in sufficient quantity. With rDNA, the gene responsible for the toxin can be isolated and inserted into the DNA of a cell that is easy to maintain. The cell can be instructed to activate the gene and cause it to begin producing the desired toxin, with both the efficiencies and economies required for C/B warfare applications.

An added advantage of this biotechnology process is that a desired toxic agent need not be mass produced far in advance of when it is needed. Once the cell is produced, cultures can be stored and only activated when needed, and this need not be done in the same location where the cell was developed. A cell culture can easily be transported to a different region of the world where relatively unskilled but adequately instructed personnel can then use the cell culture to manufacture a large quantity of the desired toxin in a few days' time.

A common bacteria, for example *Escherichia coli*, the friendly intestinal inhabitant, is now being used in precisely this way: to manufacture toxins for research. In this manner, *E. Coli* or other common bacteria can also be turned into biological warfare agents by implanting in them the gene that produces diseases such as cholera, or typhus, or diphtheria. This is not merely hypothetical; it has already been done successfully and described in the scientific literature.

Many diseases would make devastating biological warfare agents. But these diseases are presently "unsuitable" agents because of their vulnerability to normal environmental conditions (such as sunlight, temperature, or moisture); to the body's immune system; or to antibiotics. Using rDNA technology, the diseases' pathogens can be genetically manipulated to eliminate these "disadvantages." Survivability can be built in, along with resistance to anticipated methods of treatment. The organism also can be modified to escape detection or proper diagnosis under most normal situations. As a specific example, consider anthrax, which would be one of the best natural biological warfare agents, were it not for the fact that anthrax spores live for decades and hence render uninhabitable any area where they have been employed. This problem can now be solved by selecting an asporogenous (nonspore forming) mutant. This has already been done for commercial applications with the closely related bacteria *Bacillus thuringiensis*.

The second basic genetic engineering technique developed in the mid-1970s is the production of monoclonal antibodies (MCAs). Antibodies are proteins that recognize and bind to foreign substances in our bodies, such as disease cells, and therefore form a critical element in our immune system. In 1976, cells responsible for the production of antibodies were fused with hardy cancerous cells that enabled the antibody-producing cells to live and function in a laboratory outside the parent organs in which they had previously functioned. The married cells were called hybridomas. These hybridomas produce antibodies that otherwise are very difficult to obtain in quantity. By producing antibodies in quantity, MCAs facilitate critical research on the operation of the immune system. A natural consequence of this knowledge is the ability to defeat the immune system.

The devastating implications of this knowledge, coupled with the techniques of genetic engineering, raise a particularly horrifying new dimension with respect to the art of the possible in high-tech biological warfare. Not only can one construct "infective agents against which no credible defense is possible," the warning voiced by Nobel laureate biochemist Joshua Lederberg in the early 1970s, but one can also construct agents that attack critical components of the immune system and render the body vulnerable to a wide spectrum of both common and unusual diseases. The problems associated with responding to such a possibility can be observed in the growing AIDS epidemic.

Because antibodies are devilishly selective, they are designed to attach to very specific molecular structures, and can be used as vehicles to carry toxins to specific cells in the body. For example, an antibody is developed to attack a particular protein receptor that is part of the target cell. Then a toxin is attached to the antibody. In this manner, toxins can be placed in very specific locations, that is, where they can kill specific cells and produce very specific results. This operation also has been performed and described in the scientific literature.

A related area of investigation is neuropharmacology. In the study of the brain and its control of both psychological and physiological processes, certain cells have been found that produce small quantities of chemicals that are extremely critical to the regulation of various biological processes and to mental health. One example of such chemicals is the set of neurotransmitters that are essential for intercellular communications. Through modern biochemical techniques, scientists have developed an ever-increasing ability to design and synthesize chemicals that can interfere with the natural production of these neurotransmitters, or with the receptors that act in their presence—and thus sabotage the intercellular communication system. Because such chemicals are designed to have a specific affinity for a very specific cell or chemical, their effective toxicities are extremely high; only pico- or nanograms are required on the part of an aggressor to disable an intended victim and to do so in an extremely sophisticated and selective manner.

The new "designer drugs" that became popular in California in the early 1980s provide an insight into the type of sophisticated chemical agent design that is now possible. New substances have been synthesized to mimic heroin, but in a far more efficient and devastating way. Indeed, the current (or second) generation of such drugs is about four thousand times stronger than heroin. The designer's ability is so sophisticated that within a few weeks after a new black-market drug is obtained, identified, and specified to be illegal by the appropriate government authorities, the designer is able to produce a new drug that is slightly different from the earlier model, and hence not illegal, but that has the same or even enhanced effect on the user. These modified constructs are called analogues. Through the design and production of analogues, the drug designer not only stays ahead of the law, but simultaneously increases the effectiveness of the product. And though such drugs are intended to enhance an individual's ability to escape into a world of pleasure or hallucinations, one can posit the application of similar techniques to altering learning, memory, thinking, perception, coordination of motor activities, mood, and other behavioral characteristics. Moreover, minute, undetectable quantities of such chemicals could be inserted into the normal stream of recreational drugs by those people who control the trafficking infrastructure or supply the raw material, and no one would know.

A related area of research involves neurotoxins that attack the nervous system and brain in various ways. For example, they can induce rapid loss of consciousness or paralysis. These toxins are generally very complex proteins that can be subdivided to isolate small segments, or active sites, that are ultimately responsible for the physiological effect. One legitimate goal of this research is to develop more effective anesthesia. Another legitimate goal is the development of more effective tranquilizers and psychotherapy drugs. Alternatively, this work can lead to the development of extremely effective incapacitants of the type that might be used to put large urban regions to sleep or to dull the senses of specific decisionmakers or provide them with a false sense of euphoria.

Certain neurotoxins affect the mind and behavioral characteristics in more subtle ways. In this case research will provide additional knowledge of how specific chemicals affect the brain and enable the development of small-molecular-weight peptides that may act as tranquilizers or sedatives, or conversely, induce fear or erratic physical or mental behavior. Sophisticated chemical warfare agents of this kind could be economically manufactured with available biotechnology techniques and weaponized to attack large regions, selective areas, or even small groups. Similarly, by using rDNA techniques, organisms could be made to produce the toxic or "special effects" proteins. Then, these new biological warfare agents could be surreptitiously administered to the unsuspecting target in food, water, or a simple cocktail.

Perhaps one of the most serious difficulties growing out of the aforementioned possibilities is identifying when an attack has actually taken place. How do you know when a person's behavior or mental processes have been externally influenced? This problem would be especially pronounced during a crisis. The simple answer is that at present there is no way of knowing. Except in the crudest situations, such as placing LSD in the coffee urn, no one has even begun to consider the problem.

Notwithstanding the enormous impact of the new techniques such as DNA, protein sequencing, and peptide synthesis, it would be a mistake to assume that the more traditional and commonplace organisms or techniques are now obsolete for biological warfare. Much to the contrary, they also have benefited from the broad scientific advances of the past decade. Recent developments in modern microbiology have increased our understanding of classic diseases and traditional organisms and our ability to use them for malevolent purposes. Dissemination of microorganisms, traditionally a problem in biological warfare, can be achieved quite easily today through aerosolization. Modern freeze-drying and microencapsulation techniques can be employed to increase survivability. And diseases that are sensitive to sunlight, such as tularemia and plague, can be aerosolized following encapsulation. New and interesting diseases have been found; through what are now regarded as conventional techniques, strains of diseases can be developed that are resistant to the anticipated treatment.

One of the more effective approaches to the selection of potent agents is the identification of new diseases (for example Legionnaires' disease) and new subtypes of viruses—especially the latter. These new subtypes develop quite naturally as the result of natural genetic instability. Developing such strains and the antibodies for one's own population could be a natural military medical research objective. Because of the absence of immunity to a new subtype virus, when one arises it usually leads to a massive epidemic. The worldwide influenza outbreak of 1918–19 remains a good example of how deadly a simple virus can be. As many as fifty million people were killed by the virulent strains that circled the globe several times during that period. In Philadelphia alone, forty-five hundred people perished in one week from the virus. So serious was the outbreak that bodies were piled on the sidewalks of Pennsylvania Avenue in front of the White House until they could be disposed of. An epidemic of such dimensions, which today could be deliberated manufactured by a hostile adversary, might paralyze a nation for months, even years, and the real cause might never be known.

Such possibilities are only the tip of the proverbial iceberg. They are, however, adequate to illustrate how extensive and astounding the current revolution in the life sciences is and why many people believe this revolution will eclipse the Industrial Revolution in terms of reshaping the contemporary world. Propelled by the engine of scientific discovery, the revolution continues to gather momentum, and there is no end in sight. And though the potential for good is truly unlimited, the potential for evil is equally great.

Scenario Seven: Rhein–Main Air Force Base, West Germany

Bernie Jacobs had been working almost seventy-two hours without more than a couple of catnaps, and he was exhausted. Despite the long hours, he was no further ahead than when he started and that was frustrating. Damn frustrating.

The hospital laboratory, located at Rhein–Main Air Force Base in West Germany, was a beehive of activity, with dozens of doctors and technicians poring over microscopes and other equipment. Dr. Jacobs had just been flown over in a jet fighter from Atlanta, where he worked on research relating to infectious diseases at the Centers for Disease Control. The trip over had been one of the most exciting experiences of his life, in contrast to the drudgery of the work in which he was now engaged.

He had hardly begun work in Atlanta when two uniformed military officers had showed up at his office and told him the "Blue Team" had been activated, and that he was to come with them. The Blue Team had been formed two years earlier to deal with national threats of a chemical or biological nature, a counterpart organization to the Nuclear Emergency Search Team (NEST). He had been driven straight to the airport where the jet was already on the tarmac waiting for him. He hadn't even had time to call his wife until he reached Europe to say he wouldn't be home for dinner.

It was not the greatest time to be in Europe, reflected Jacobs, with the threat of war in the air. The Soviets had rolled across the border into Iran a week earlier: U.S. and NATO forces were now on full alert. Diplomatic efforts to defuse the crisis did not seem to be leading anywhere. There was a very real possibility that U.S. and other allied military forces might be landed in Iran to block the Soviet drive to the Persian Gulf, and it could only be speculated that that would precipitate a shooting war in the region that would be difficult to contain.

However, there couldn't be any opposition to the Soviets, Jacobs knew, if U.S. readiness couldn't be dramatically improved in the next several days. Indeed, U.S. military forces in Europe and the Mediterranean had been devastated by a severe gastrointestinal epidemic that had appeared two weeks earlier. Some units were at less than 50-percent strength. Whole air wings were in sick bay, and hospitals could not handle all the new cases. The U.S. Carrier Task Force, steaming toward the Persian Gulf, was now being hit with the epidemic and cables from the fleet indicated that "men were falling like flies."

The weird thing about the particular bug that was causing all the trouble was that no one had yet been able to isolate it, and hence identify it, which was what Jacobs had been flown over to do. In view of the severity of the political crisis, he had been given every resource he wanted; all he had to do was issue a command. But, despite unlimited resources and a staff of more than fifty, he still hadn't come up with anything.

"Maybe it's from outer space," quipped one of the technicians, a redhead from Kansas named Sally. "Remember that film The Andromeda Strain? *Maybe that's what we're dealing with."*

"I'm almost ready to believe it," said Jacobs, wiping the sweat from his brow. "Damn," he muttered to himself. "Why can't we isolate it, whatever the hell it is?"

In all of his experience as an epidemiologist, he had never encountered anything like it. Sure, there had been plenty of perplexing cases, but nothing where there was so much sickness yet so few data to work with. The symptoms of the illness were not unlike those connected with a severe case of stomach flu, although this bug appeared to be resistant to all standard antibiotics. More disturbing, however, was the rising mortality rate following the onset of symptoms that had many of the clinical manifestations of cholera. But, if it was cholera, where was the causative organism, the Vibrio cholerae, *that should be evident in the stool samples of those afflicted?*

It wasn't until his friend and colleague, Dr. Lacey Davis, arrived on the scene that answers began falling into place. Over nonstop cups of coffee late into the night, they reviewed all of the laboratory and clinical data that had been accumulated.

"Well?" *asked Bernie, looking drawn and tired, as Lacey digested the last of the material piled high atop the table.* "We've done everything by the book. We haven't missed a thing in my judgment. And yet we still don't have a clue to what it is."

Lacey pushed back the long strands of auburn hair that kept falling into her face and rubbed her eyes, which were red from a combination of jet lag and hours of poring over the volumes of data on the table. She had been a professor of internal medicine at Harvard Medical School before joining the Centers for Disease Control, and Bernie knew that she had one of the best medical investigative minds in the United States.

"Maybe that's just it," *she said at last.* "You've done everything by the book. Have you considered the possibility that someone might have engineered a bug so that standard medical diagnostic practices wouldn't work? Could it be that we're dealing with something not natural but man-made, and that it was designed by people who counted on us using predictable medical research techniques to find it?"

"What are you saying?" *Bernie demanded with irritation.* "That the Russians are behind it? Come on, give me a break. You're beginning to sound like Sally."

"Who?"

"Oh, one of the research technicians. She thinks it may have come from outer space," *he said mockingly.*

"The one thing this work demands is an open mind," *retorted Lacey angrily.* "A willingness to seek answers anywhere, to test every hypothesis no matter how far-fetched. What I'm suggesting may be a long shot, but do you have any better ideas?"

The fact that the outbreak of the illness coincided with the Soviet push into Iran had not gone unnoticed. But, if the Soviets were behind it, Jacobs asked himself, how did they do it?

"If you were to genetically engineer a bug so no one could find it, one that wouldn't grow in the usual broth or agar plate media used by clinical diagnosticians," *asked Lacey, trying to think like a Soviet biological warfare specialist,* "what would you do?"

"I guess I would engineer it to grow in a different medium or at a different temperature," he responded reluctantly.

"Exactly," she said. "Let's run the experiments again, only this time we'll change both the medium and the temperature. We need a full scan on both."

While Jacobs returned to the laboratory to get the new experiments under way, Davis collapsed on a couch in a nearby office. She was awakened from a deep sleep hours later by Jacobs. Gazing groggily up into his smiling face, she rubbed her eyes and tried to shake the cobwebs from her brain.

"You were right," he announced. "It won't grow at either the usual temperature or in the usual medium. But . . . change the temperature and medium, and bingo! It pops right up."

Lacey bolted to her feet, and Bernie directed her to a microscope in the laboratory.

"It appears to be a strange species of E. coli *that grows at a temperature somewhere between thirty-one and thirty-two degrees centigrade, instead of a thirty-seven.*" Thirty-seven degrees centigrade is the normal body temperature, Lacey knew, and therefore the temperature at which virtually all diagnostic laboratories grow their cultures.

"And what was the growth medium on this slide?"

"Lactose."

"So that's why some people get it and others don't. Cunning bastards, aren't they," Lacey concluded bitterly.

"Forgive me for being such a jerk," he said, planting a sloppy wet kiss on her cheek. "I owe you one."

"How about dinner when this nightmare is over?"

"You're on." But instead of basking in the warm flow of success, the smile died on his lips, and he added: "If this 'nightmare' ever is over."

Less than a day later, Jacobs was presenting their findings to the NATO high command.

"In summary, then, we now believe that the Soviets have engineered a new, highly sophisticated bacterium as a biological warfare weapon. Using a species of E. coli, *they altered it so that it could be dumped into any standard water system and withstand the effects of normal chlorination long enough to do the job, and short enough not to leave any evidence in the water. Once ingested, it does not grow until it reaches the small intestine. Growth itself is triggered when the bacteria combine with lactose. Thus, those people who had ingested milk or other dairy products came down with the illness, while those who didn't usually escaped infection. Not only did it not grow in the usual media used to cultivate bacteria,"* Jacobs continued, shaking his head, *"but they attempted to throw us off the trail even further by engineering it to grow under standard culture practices at a temperature far lower than doctors and hospital microbiologists are accustomed to using. To grow it at a normal thirty-seven degrees centigrade would have required the introduction of intestinal fluid, something no physician or researcher could have known."* Jacobs paused and tried to find the right words to convey the enormity of the situation. *"Gentlemen, the age of gene warfare has just dawned, and it is potentially a far more dramatic watershed than Hiroshima."*

Soviet Military Interest
in Biochem Agent Technology

The classic U.S. military scenario involving chemical warfare takes place in Europe. The Warsaw Pact launches a massive conventional attack against NATO forces. Subsequently, Warsaw Pact forces begin mass strikes with chemical warfare agents; short persistent agents that dissipate rapidly are used near the front and longer persistent agents are used in the rear areas. Near the front, nerve agents, usually sarin, are delivered by tube artillery or multiple-rocket launchers. For targets in the rear, airplanes or medium-range missiles (such as FROG and SCUD missiles) delivering mustard or VX, or the semipersistent nerve agent soman, are used. Since the Afghanistan war, helicopters and mycotoxins occasionally enter into the scenario.

A massive application of chemical agents (as outlined) would rapidly reduce NATO military actions to slow motion, in spite of the billions of dollars that have been spent on chemical warfare defenses over the past ten years. Though such defensive measures may have improved the survivability of NATO forces, nevertheless they do little to enable them to continue fighting. Try as it might, the military has not yet learned how to fight in a contaminated environment. Chemical weapons make war fighting exceedingly difficult.

Not only is this scenario intensely discouraging, but it employs technology that is over twenty years old. With the possible exception of the use of helicopters, all of the armaments and agents in the classic U.S. scenario were in the Soviet stockpile before 1965. Indeed, most of them date back to the mid-1950s and earlier. None of the scenarios currently in use by U.S. military planners consider biological agents or the types of high-tech biochem agents discussed in the preceding two chapters.

Is it wise, one might ask, to assume that the Warsaw Pact forces have not introduced any substantial improvements into their forces in over twenty years? We think not, especially considering their R&D objectives in the 1960s and the major expansion of their C/B warfare facilities and capabilities that has been taking place continuously since the mid-1960s. Or, conversely, what are the types of improvements that should be considered now in assessing the nature of the Warsaw Pact threat?

The two most likely improvements from the Soviet perspective are better agents and better agent packaging. With respect to better agents, the desire for increased lethality would be a top priority. Additionally, interest in achieving a persistent vapor threat (one lasting several hours to several days) is logical. Current agents such as sarin and soman are effective, but only for a short period of time (several minutes). The problem with sarin was pointed out in 1984 congressional testimony during which U.S. Air Force General Charles L. Donnelly, Jr., described the disadvantage of nonpersistent sarin bombs: "Two hundred feet away from impact, one could virtually hold his breath until it dissipates." Persistent agents such as VX will contaminate an area for several days, but the vapor hazard following an attack also only lasts for a very short time (while the material is falling to the ground), after which the vapor hazard rapidly drops to near zero.

Microencapsulation is another technology that has seen major improvements since the mid-1970s. This technology could be used to facilitate the timed release of volatile agents. It also could be employed to produce particles the size and weight of which could be selected in advance to optimize their depositions. A likely target of Soviet research efforts is the two-stage microcapsule. This is a large microcapsule designed to penetrate the atmospheric inversion layers and to fall rapidly to the ground in predictable patterns. Inside the large microcapsule are many smaller capsules containing different agents with different agent release rates.

Microencapsulation was one of the technical fields the U.S. Army was interested in shortly before its research took a tailspin in 1969. As early as 1967, numerous advantages had been identified, including reduction of toxic agent handling hazards; particle presizing; stabilization by isolation; protection from light or other hostile environments; sustained release; and dissemination upon impact. Such advantages, incidentally, are as applicable to biological agents as they are to chemical agents. Since that time, the technology has greatly advanced. Obvious applications that are now in commercial use include time-release capsules; encapsulated organisms for research and insect control; impact-release capsules (for example "scratch 'n sniff" magazine inserts); and a wide variety of encapsulated essences (ideal for sabotage purposes).

It defies credulity that the many advantages of microencapsulation to C/B warfare would have gone unnoticed by the Soviets. Indeed, events in Southeast Asia indicate that the Soviets may have been experimenting with microcapsules. The use of "bluish-green egglike objects" in Laos has been reported by numerous refugees. Surface moisture that the large capsules came in contact with caused them to disintegrate, exposing a black core that gave off noxious fumes.

Microcapsules for insect control permit the timed release of insecticides. A similar development that would extend the duration of chemical agent contamination is of obvious military use. Microcapsules sized to behave as dust or pollen would be far more effective than aerosols (which tend to dissipate rapidly) in extending the contamination time. Microencapsulation of this type could also be designed to confuse or deny sensor detection, and possibly even to provide both delayed reaction following inhalation and entrapment in the human respiratory system. The production of particles of this size was possible in 1967, although they were a bit large for passing through filters (one to ten microns). Smaller-sized particles are well within the state of the art today.

The timed or extended release of agents need not provide for lethal contaminant levels. Very low sublethal levels, even below those readily detectable with available sensors, may be even more useful in terms of their overall effect on personnel readiness and military capability. Far too much emphasis in the West is placed on lethality. Nonlethal doses can be militarily more effective because sick or disabled soldiers and dependents tie up scarce resources, demand the energies of those still healthy, and have a very demoralizing effect.

Special attention should be given to incapacitants that are now believed to have taken on increased military significance in Soviet strategy. There are reports that in the mid-1970s Soviet military exercises had written into the script the mock employment of incapacitants. These were designed to temporarily disable the population of large urban areas so that military operations could proceed unimpeded. In one case, the mock use of incapacitating agents immobilized a Western European port (Copenhagen) while the Soviet Army established firm control over the port facilities.

The Soviet use of C/B weapons for urban warfare must also be anticipated. Europe, with its dense population, is an obvious example where such use would be logical. Urban warfare is exceedingly difficult, time-consuming, and costly. C/B weapons that could clear or neutralize large urban areas in short periods of time (in hours or days) would be a highly valued element of Warsaw Pact capability. Delivery of the desired agents could be by plane, missile, or multiple-rocket launchers. Military vehicles used to lay down smoke screens, or even cars with hidden internal aerosol generators, could be driven through target cities disseminating C/B agents. In essence, this is precisely what has been taking place in Southeast Asia and Afghanistan, although in a rural village context. Chemical and toxin agents are being used against Afghan villages to force residents out of their homes and into refugee camps, thus ending their ability to provide clandestine support to the mujahadeen. The same techniques could be employed in a war against an industrialized or urbanized nation, the only exception being that different agents would likely be used.

There are also reports of Soviet employment of rapid-acting incapacitants in Afghanistan. According to a European chemical warfare specialist, this was inadvertently referred to in a State Department report as having involved rapid-acting "lethal" agents. Whether lethal or not, the reported rapidity of the agents was unprecedented. The incapacitants allegedly acted so fast that people were "frozen" in fixed positions. There are also stories of people who awoke after several hours with no recollection that anything had happened. Time had simply been stolen from them.

It seems almost certain that the creation of a variety of incapacitating agents would be a major objective of any Soviet C/B warfare development program. One can envision agents ranging from those that totally immobilize their victims (putting them under the effects of a powerful anesthesia) to agents that merely render a large group of people unperturbed by what is taking place around them (in other words, mass tranquilization). It is also not difficult to imagine interest in a variety of agents that would excite certain emotional behavior, such as fear, in crowds or major population segments. These types of effects would seem more interesting from a sabotage or terrorist point of view, rather than from a military operations perspective. The possible Soviet interest in "control incapacitants" is clearly reflected in the writings of communist-bloc scientists referred to earlier, and in the observations of Soviet émigrés with respect to the psychiatric practices that are widely employed in the Soviet Union. The possibility is also suggested in a Soviet text on military toxicology, which states that the United States has programs for "controlling the psychic state of populations of cities and country by means of using chemical substances which cause suppression of the stimulating processes, a sense of contentment, non-resistance, susceptibility." Of course such claims are nonsense, but they clearly indicate Soviet awareness of and interest in such incapacitants.

Since 1940, the Soviets have consistently sought to develop agents that could penetrate through or otherwise defeat Western protective gas masks and garments. In this connection, several reports since the early 1980s suggest that they have succeeded in realizing this goal or at least have developed several promising possibilities. Senator Barry Goldwater, at a 28 February 1985 hearing of the Senate Armed Services Committee, stated that U.S. intelligence estimates now credit the Soviets with possessing chemical agents capable of penetrating U.S. protective gear. Both mask penetrants and explosively driven slivers, or fléchettes (which penetrate protective gear) were attributed to the Soviets by the Presidential Chemical Warfare Review Commission in June 1985.

One of the most desirable characteristics of any agent is rapid action, which is why there is so much concern over the reports of the "instant death" or the "one-breath anesthesia" that came out of Afghanistan in 1980. Fast-acting agents would be ideal agents to use against high-priority targets, such as command and control or intelligence centers. Such centers may not warrant a nuclear weapon and often are designed to withstand attacks with conventional weapons. Most facilities of this type have good air circulation that would facilitate rapid distribution of the agent throughout the center. An agent that could pass through whatever filters are in use (in many cases only the crudest types), and stop people before any remedial or offensive actions could be taken in response, is well within the current capabilities of the Soviet Union.

An intriguing assault weapon would be an Israeli Model 5 projectojet filled with a fast-acting incapacitant. This model "gas thrower" holds two kilograms of wet or dry agent that can be projected forward in a stream out to six hundred feet. The current model, filled with CS-1 suspended in CO_2, is said to achieve total incapacitation in two seconds. Such a weapon with a more potent fill might be far more effective than an assault rifle in attacking fortified positions or special facilities such as air bases or command and control facilities.

Soviet military concepts place emphasis on exploitation, that is, on taking advantage of the physical and psychological effects of weapons with immediate follow-on assaults to capture land, forces, or facilities. Immediately after firepower has been applied, troops—infantry, armor, or even airborne assault—attack to capitalize on the shock effect of the firepower and capture their objectives before the defending troops are able to recover and reorganize their defense. Though this is traditionally an artillery concept, the Soviets stress the importance of applying the concept to other means, particularly nuclear weapons. The situation would be no different with chemical weapons. An ideal chemical agent in this role would be one with a predictable duration of effectiveness. If the agent had a sharp decrease in effects, troops could attack without fear of encountering lingering debilitating aftereffects.

The Soviets are clearly interested in agents with effects that can be neutralized with respect to their own troops by means of immunization. They could thus eliminate or reduce the need to wear cumbersome protective garb, while still remaining effective against their adversary's military forces. The prospect of this type of development is very real. The Soviets view toxin weapons as the "third generation" of chemical weapons. As in the case of biological weapons, it is possible to immunize soldiers in advance to protect them from exposure to certain toxin weapons. The very potent protein toxins, such as botulinus toxin, are representative of agents of this type.

For their part, biological weapons are not generally regarded in the West as militarily useful because of the delay before the onset of their effects and what is viewed as their uncontrollability. This perspective, so prevelent among Western military planners, is twenty-five years out of date. Significant attention has been devoted to military medicine in recent years because ordinary medical problems still represent the chief threat to military readiness and cause of soldiers being out of action. Nevertheless, medical advances can be readily overwhelmed by agents produced in simple biological laboratories. Currently available technology permits the development of new disease strains that are very resistant to all forms of anticipated treatment. Further, microencapsulation can be utilized to make otherwise nonviable agents survivable and could result in unexpected diseases being inflicted on adversaries. In this connection, it would not be difficult to produce a new subtype virus that would wreak havoc on NATO forces, owing to the lack of adequate diagnostic techniques and vaccines. The unpredictable and often unacceptable delays before the target population manifests infection by an agent can be reduced to as little as a few hours, or programmed to emerge at a predetermined time, say eight to ten days in the future.

We can assume that Warsaw Pact forces possess any or all of the capabilities described in this chapter, and several not mentioned. These capabilities must be taken into account when assessing the risk to U.S. and NATO forces. The continued reliance on outdated, 1960s scenarios by U.S. military planners is an invitation to disaster.

In view of this fact, why then has there been so little effort to update U.S. assessments of the Soviet biochem warfare threat? Perhaps when the threat is cast as it traditionally has been, fewer question are raised concerning the adequacy of NATO defense posture and of the proposed U.S. offensive chemical weapons modernization program, which is also predicted on obsolete 1960s technology. Both situations are indefensible with respect to this nation's national security. But Pentagon planners appear to be afraid of the implications involved in any meaningful effort to address real U.S. deficiencies. Such action raises considerable debate over what shape the U.S. response should take. It also can be predicted that any serious attempt to fully expose Soviet biochem activities is likely to further exacerbate an already contentious U .S.–Soviet relationship.

The face of modern war: American troops wearing chemical gear in Vietnam.

News item: Harvard, Yale scientists claim "yellow rain" may be bee droppings ...

Controversy over "Yellow Rain": some critics of U.S. Government findings have gone so far as to suggest that residues are actually bee feces.

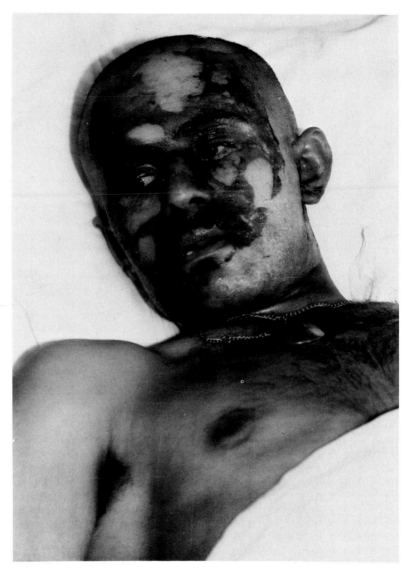

Iranian chemical weapons victim. Iraq has used chemical warfare to blunt Iranian offensives in their seven-year war. Iran is reported to have only one gas mask for every dozen soldiers.

CHEMICAL
WEAPONS

PANDORAS BOX

IRAN

IRAQ

The Christian Science Monitor

Above: Pandora's Box: as many as fifty nations will possess chemical or biological weapons by the end of the century. *Below:* A United Nations delegation confirms the use of chemical weapons by Iraq.

Above: The Israeli Model 5 projectojet, designed as a crowd control device to deliver incapacitants, could be misused by terrorists and even loaded with lethal agents. *Below:* The projectojet in use.

Scenario of a biochem attack using such a weapon on a movie theater.

Most of the world remains indifferent to the use of chemical/biological warfare by the Soviet Union and its allies.

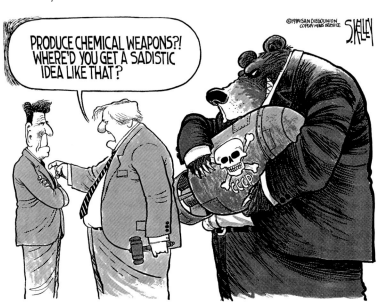

Many members of Congress do not want to confront the overwhelming evidence of Soviet treaty violations.

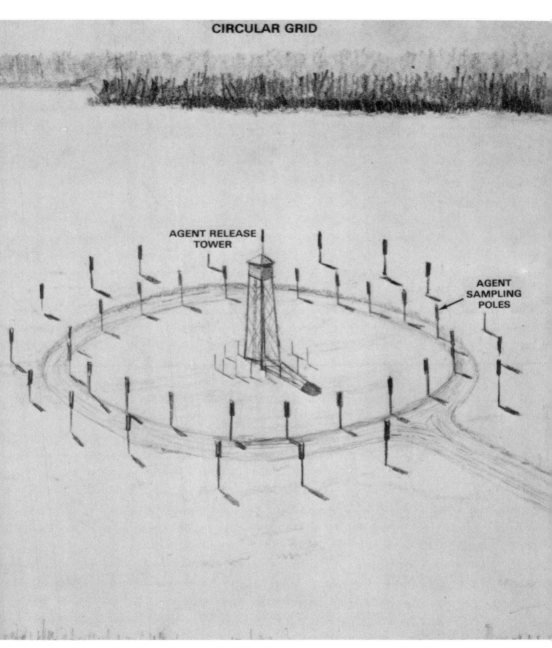

CIRCULAR GRID

AGENT RELEASE
TOWER

AGENT
SAMPLING
POLES

The Soviets reportedly test their chemical and biological agents on human
guinea pigs tied to stakes.

Above: Soviet tactical missiles, like this Scud B, can carry a chemical payload. Iran, Libya, and Syria are all reliably reported to possess Scud B missiles. *Below:* The Soviet Union and its Warsaw pact allies are far more prepared than the United States and the members of the NATO alliance to fight in a contaminated environment.

Soviet Chemical Weapons Depots, Production Centers, and Storage Areas.

Soviet chemical weapons depots are dispersed throughout the USSR.

The U.S. news media has contributed to public indifference over the Soviet biochem warfare threat.

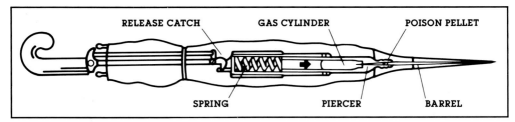

RELEASE CATCH   GAS CYLINDER   POISON PELLET

SPRING   PIERCER   BARREL

A Bulgarian exile was murdered in London by a weapon similar to this. It fires a tiny pellet containing the poison Ricin, a derivative of the lowly castor bean.

A remarkable piece of microengineering, the hollow pellet was 9/10ths platinum and 1/10th iridium. When the thin coating of wax on the pellet melted due to the body heat of the victim, it released the poison into his system.

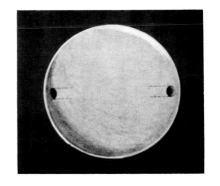

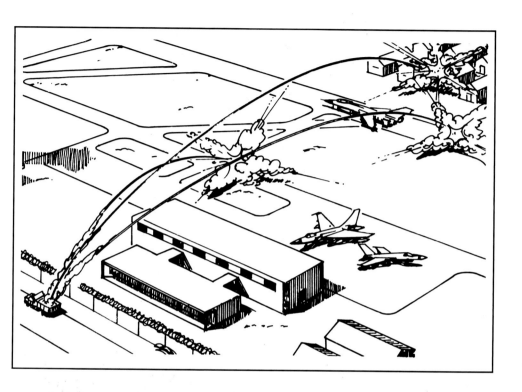

Two scenarios for carrying out a biochem attack on a U.S. airbase in Europe. *Above:* In the first, agents are dispersed over an airfield after being fired from mortar tubes buried in a truckload of sand (*right*). A similar attack, using conventional mortar rounds, was carried out by the IRA against a police facility in Northern Ireland. *Opposite page:* The second scenario illustrates an automobile surreptitiously disseminating a dried agent through a phony exhaust pipe.

Labs supplying specimen cultures are always looking for new ways to package their products. Recently a company advertised specimen cultures packaged in small flip-top cans. One biochem warfare specialist observed that all a terrorist needed was to tie a stick of dynamite to five or six cans containing a lethal agent to make a very effective weapon.

This advertisement for Ricin, a poison thousands of times more lethal than the nerve agent VX, appeared in the February 20, 1984 *Shotgun News*. Federal authorities moved quickly to shut down the operation.

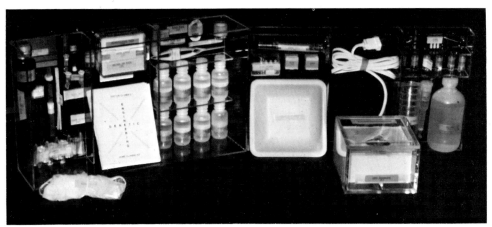

Send in the Clones—*Learn the tricks of bioengineering the way the genetic giants do—with hands-on experiments. Designed for amateur scientists age 10 and up, the kit contains all the necessities of the laboratory, including chemicals, test tubes, and other apparatus with which to make gene colonies thrive. You provide the genes—and the genius. $559.*

Biochem revolution: this advertisement of genetic engineering and gene cloning kits for children, which appeared in a 1985 Christmas catalogue, illustrates the mainstreaming of biochem warfare technology.

3
The Quiet War:
Biochem Intelligence Operations

It had bothered Myles Ackerman for some time. At first he thought it was just his imagination, but soon it was impossible to avoid the awful truth: Someone was killing the United States' leading Soviet experts and scholars. Killing those, at least, who were implacable enemies of the Soviet Union.

Initially, he attributed the premature and "accidental" deaths of so many experts in one field simply to coincidence and back luck. There was, after all, nothing to suggest foul play in the many autopsies and death certificates he had reviewed: Dr. Mars X. Imlaw, "cardiac arrest"; Dr. Dimitri Orlov, "cardiac arrest"; Dr. Catherine K. Rader, "auto accident brought on by apparent stroke"; Dr. Lloyd Rubin, "pneumonia"; Boris Mesvinski, "respiratory failure"; Dr. Ivan A. Dalokow, "cardiac arrest"; and on and on.

Then he began to dig deeper and a pattern started to emerge. What had begun as mere curiosity on Myles's part soon became an obsession. It had all begun six months earlier when he had taken the morning off from his job as a reporter for the Boston Globe *to attend the funeral of his girlfriend's father, Dr. Ivan A. Dalokow. He hadn't known Dr. Dalokow well—a dour and brooding man whose dark countenance was attributed to his youth in Russia— but he had gone to the funeral to be of whatever comfort he could to Nadia, Dalokow's daughter.*

As they had walked away from the gravesite, a woman had stopped Nadia to express her condolences. "It's so sad. All the best are gone. He was one of the last. It's almost as if God didn't want us to know the truth."

"What did she mean?" Myles asked after the woman had left.

"My father was part of a small and shrinking circle of Soviet scholars around the country who distrusted the communists, who didn't support the notion of détente," Nadia explained sadly. "He and the others saw the Soviets for what they are: thugs, gangsters. But, tragically, my father and most of the others are now dead, cut down in their prime by disease and accidents. Now there's no one left to carry on. All we will hear from in the future are the naive idealists and fellow travelers."

He had returned to his office and what seemed like his two-hundredth story on local corruption. But he was haunted by the words of the woman at the gravesite: "It's almost as if God didn't want us to know the truth." If only to put his mind to rest, he began researching the deaths of Soviet scholars around the country during the past two decades. As he documented case histories, it became clear that the death of each individual either eliminated a persistent critic of the USSR or left a vacancy that was filled by a more accommodationist scholar. Thus, over a twenty-year period, the orientation of the nation's leading Soviet studies departments and research institutes had been drastically altered. And the quality of the scholarship declined as did the number of students taking doctorates in Soviet studies. The previous year, only one Ph.D. was awarded in Soviet studies at U.S. institutions of higher learning. The United States was slowly and inexorably becoming blind about its major adversary.

Still, he had no proof, just a lot of circumstantial evidence, nothing to prove a massive conspiracy designed to manipulate U.S. attitudes about the Soviet Union.

Finally, the break came that he needed. Nadia and her mother granted him permission to have Dr. Dalakow's remains exhumed and an autopsy performed. With Nadia's help he also secured permission from three of the families of other deceased Soviet scholars to exhume their remains for new autopsies. Performed by a specialist in forensic medicine and a well-known toxicologist, the new autopsies revealed startling evidence that the scholars were murdered and had not died of natural causes. A tiny fléchette was found in the back of Dr. Dalakow's neck. It was so small that Dalokow probably felt no more sensation than that of a mosquito bite. An analysis of the poison residue found in the fléchette revealed that shellfish toxin (known as saxitoxin, which is produced by certain plankton) was the real cause of death. Myles learned later that special firearms had been developed by Soviet intelligence to fire such fléchettes.

Shellfish toxin was also used to murder Dr. Orlov. He had died unexpectedly while attending a conference, and his personal effects had been mailed to his wife who, fortunately, had not opened the box but simply stuck it away on a shelf in a closet. A check of his personal effects found telltale signs of the toxin mixed in a bottle of after-shave lotion. Undamaged skin offers total protection to toxins, but a small cut would permit the toxin to penetrate easily. Shaving often causes enough small wounds for toxins to penetrate.

Traces of prussic acid (or hydrogen cyanide), a blood gas toxin, were found in Boris Mesvinski's tissues. More than likely he had been sprayed in the face with the chemical in liquid form, producing rapid paralysis of the brain's respiratory center, causing death within minutes. It was an old Soviet assassination method.

Dr. Rader's case was more difficult. Gradually an answer emerged as the autopsy indicated that there was an extremely high probability that she had been killed by means of a nerve agent— DMSO mixture. DMSO, by itself, is often described as a "miracle drug" that purportedly gives relief to many arthritis sufferers. But DMSO is a remarkable transmittal agent. Myles learned about tests conducted on rabbits at Edgewood Arsenal where droplets of VX– DMSO were placed on the skin of the test animals. Because of the absorbent properties of DMSO, it took only half as long for the test animals to die when the VX–DMSO mixture was used than when pure VX was used. Myles and his colleagues conjectured that the nerve agent–DMSO compound had been smeared on the steering wheel or door handle of Dr. Rader's car. As the agent was absorbed through her fingers and palms, it caused her to have a stroke-like seizure while at the wheel of the car. When she blacked out, the car crashed and she lost her life.

"How could so many mistakes have been made in the original autopsies?" Myles asked Dr. Bernard Gold, the forensic medicine specialist.

"A high index of suspicion is required to reject what appears to be the obvious cause of death," replied Gold. "Unless the doctors have some reason to believe otherwise, they are not going to search further for a cause of death than cardiac arrest or stroke when all of the signs in the deceased point to that conclusion."

On a trip to Washington, an old friend who worked for the CIA yielded the final piece of the puzzle: the question of who was behind the murders and for what purpose. Myles's friend described what was known as Service A within the First Main Directorate of the KGB. This directorate is charged with responsibility for foreign operations, and Service A handles so-called active measures, which is the Soviet term for "influence operations" in the West. He also explained that next to foreign counterintelligence organizations, the directorate's top priority was given to organizations and individuals engaged in the study of the Soviet Union. This is a logical result of the massive Soviet disinformation and deception operation whose goal is to control the West's perceptions the Soviet Union.

Over the next few weeks, a picture gradually emerged, despite his attempt to suppress it, to put it out of mind. Every indicator suggested that the USSR was systematically killing leading U.S. Sovietologists. It was doing so to eliminate both those who understood too well the true nature of the Soviet Union and its policies, and those who stood in the way of the advancement of scholars whose views the Soviets found compatible with the misperceptions they hoped to foster in the West. It was a plot so insidious that it took Myles's breath away. This was the stuff of spy novels, he wanted to believe, not the real world. But he knew that he wasn't imagining it; too many pieces of the puzzle were falling into place.

For three weeks he cloistered himself in his Boston apartment, working on the story that he knew was the biggest of his career—page one, Pulitzer prize stuff. As he polished the final draft, he was interrupted by a knock on his apartment door. Through the peephole, he spied a well-dressed woman in her thirties.

"Yes?" he said, through a small crack in the door.

"Can you tell me where Penny Murray lives?" asked the woman in a pleasant voice.

Disarmed by her smile and sweet manner, Myles opened the door and stepped out into the hall so that he could point out Penny Murray's apartment.

Out of the corner of his eye he caught a glimpse of what looked like a child's water pistol in her hand, then he felt the warm liquid on his face, in his eyes, nostrils, and throat. There was an instant of recognition, before he collapsed, that the liquid was prussic acid.

The coroner attributed his death to respiratory failure. No trace of his research was ever found.

Wet Operations

The most glaring deficiency in the manner in which the C/B threat is perceived by U.S. military and intelligence services is their lack of attention to nonbattlefield applications.

C/B warfare is seen almost exclusively as a tactical battlefield problem that is of concern exclusively to military commanders stationed in Europe. But while those problems are, indeed, extremely severe, they represent only a small segment of the C/B problem, and quite possibly the least important segment.

One of the most important dimensions of C/B warfare is its use as an effective instrument by Soviet and Eastern European intelligence services since the early 1960s. These intelligence operations are of two different forms, so-called "wet" operations (or active measures undertaken for political reasons during "peacetime") and sabotage (or *spetsnaz*) operations undertaken for political or military reasons on the eve of war.

Wet operations are an ongoing reality of modern East–West relations, and one that Western nations are most reluctant to confront, or even acknowledge. They include the use of C/B agents for assassinations; intimidation and coercion; compromise and blackmail; kidnapping; and neutralization. Soviet targets routinely include Western diplomats and politicians; dissidents; individuals who have fled various totalitarian regimes; journalists; and anti-Soviet scholars. As an example of these activities, in the summer of 1985 alone, wet operations involving chemical agents were identified and reported in the media on three separate occasions: chemical "spy dust" used to track U.S. diplomats and their contacts in Moscow; the drugging and kidnapping of a Soviet defector who had become a naturalized U.S. citizen; and the drugging and intimidation of a Soviet seaman attempting to defect.

Perhaps the most serious Soviet wet operations are political assassinations. In what might seem like a chapter from a James Bond novel, the Soviets have drawn upon a varied and sophisticated arsenal of exotic C/B weapons to murder their enemies. Soviet agents generally seek to make such assassinations appear as though the victim died of natural causes. Such efforts are euphemistically referred to among Soviet intelligence agents as giving the target a "case of the measles." In 1957, Captain Nikolai Khokhlov, a Soviet defector, was poisoned, presumably by the KGB, using tiny, highly radioactive metal fragments that were slipped into his food. Two years later, Stefan Bandera, a Ukrainian exile, died when prussic acid was sprayed in his face.

Two well-publicized chemical assassination attempts occurred in 1978 when a pair of Bulgarian exiles—one living in London, the other in Paris—were attacked by assailants using the umbrellas that fired microscopic pellets containing the deadly poison ricin. The London victim, Georgi Markov, died, but his countryman in Paris, Vladimir Kostov, was more fortunate. French doctors found the tiny pellet (a remarkable piece of microengineering and biotechnology made of an exotic alloy of iridium and platinum) in Kostov's back. It had lodged in the subcutaneous fat layer and was surgically removed in time to save his life. The ricin is kept in place by a wax that melts at normal body temperature. Fortunately for Kostov, the heat in the fat layer was insufficient to melt the wax before the surgeons were able to remove the pellet.

Intelligence sources in the West say that a similar pellet-firing weapon has been responsible for at least six assassinations in recent years, including a CIA double agent, Boris Korczak, who was hit at Tyson's Corner, Virginia. Korczak was rushed to Fairfax hospital, where a major fight developed between the CIA and the Soviets over custody of the body. The CIA held off the Soviets until the cause of Korczak's death was fixed, which turned out to be a small platinum-iridium pellet, which presumably contained ricin. The CIA got the pellet; the Soviets got the body, which they immediately shipped to Russia on an Aeroflot plane from which all passengers were excluded. Ironically, the ricin toxin umbrella weapon might be the offspring or copy of a similar U.S. pellet weapon (developed for use with saxitoxin or ricin) that was publicized during the 1976 Church Committee hearings on CIA activities.

The Soviets and their satellites have numerous assassination weapon factories. As reported by Anatoli Golitzyn, a KGB officer who defected in 1961, the KGB was reorganized in the late 1950s into two main directorates, intelligence and counterintelligence. At that time, there remained four main services, one of which was exclusively devoted to the production of poisons for assassinations required in support of policy.

Jan Sejna reported that within the Eastern-bloc satellites, most of the development of assassination poisons was performed in Bulgaria and East Germany during the early 1960s. Then, in 1965, Czechoslovak intelligence was given a major role in developing assassination weapons and techniques. An institute dedicated to the research and development of assassination and neutralization weapons was formed. A factory located in Hostivar, a suburb of Prague, was turned over to military intelligence for the actual production of the weapons. Many top scientists were involved in the project, and C/B weapons were among the highest-priority development programs. One of the more widely publicized examples of biological weapons used in assassinations is the unusual sickness and death in 1963 of the British Labour party leader Hugh Gaitskell after he ate biscuits and tea at the Soviet Embassy. A second example is the 1978 assassination of the popular Algerian leader, Houari Boumédienne. Authoritative sources have linked his death to exotic biological agents injected with the same platinum–iridium pellet gun used against the Bulgarian dissidents in 1978.

In order to recruit, intimidate, or simply discredit a person, the Soviets will drug him or her, and then either place the person in an incriminating situation (usually sexual), or in an embarrassing situation (drunken rowdiness, incompetent espionage, or public behavior not fitting an officer). This has repeatedly happened to "un-friendly enemies," for example military attachés, unsympathetic journalists, and security personnel while serving in or visiting the Soviet Union and other communist countries.

In the early 1960s, a single woman journalist developed a num-ber of male Soviet friends and frequently attended parties as the only foreigner. On one occasion, she was drugged. The next day, pictures of her unclothed (and carefully staged as if she had passed out from drinking) appeared in the Soviet press as a warning that she was not to associate with Soviet citizens.

A Western European correspondent suffered a similar assault. One evening, shortly after his return from a trip to Central Asia, he was seated at a table with a Soviet male. They engaged in conver-sation and had several drinks. The correspondent soon became un-conscious. The next morning he woke up, nude, in bed, with Soviet photographers around. He was not permitted to leave the room. Soon a person entered with pictures that showed him in bed with his dinner companion of the previous evening, committing sexual acts. Unless he was willing to cooperate in the future with certain Soviets, the pictures would be shown to his wife.

In 1964 the West Germans were tipped off by a defector that the Soviets had planted listening devices throughout the West Ger-man Embassy in Moscow. A West German electronics engineer, Horst Schwirkmann, was sent to perform a thorough "sweep" of the embassy. After completing his work and finding numerous So-viet bugs, he was taken by a fellow countryman to Zagorsk, an attraction for foreign tourists about seventy kilometers north of Moscow. He later recalled feeling a sharp prick in his leg while they were sightseeing. Shortly thereafter, he experienced severe pain. His companion took him to the U.S. Embassy where a doctor was avail-able, and it was discovered that the Soviets had apparently shot him with a dart, containing mustard, in retribution for his efficiency (and as an example to others).

This was not a one-time event. The same modus operandi, but using drugs rather than mustard, was reported in 1971. This time the targets were two Japanese electronics specialists who had been sent to Moscow to perform a detailed sweep of their embassy for electronic bugs. On this occasion, the drug employed was not lethal, but rather was designed to make its targets very ill.

Most often such incidents tend to be ignored, even surpressed, especially when U.S. officials are targeted. These incidents are accepted as a condition of doing business with the Soviets. Neither the Defense Intelligence Agency (DIA) nor the State Department are known to keep records of such provocations. Specific incidents are discussed in whispers; the less said the better. Worse still, the blame is often placed on the victim. As described by a former U.S. defense attaché, "Whenever an American in Moscow is drugged, the individual somehow is judged guilty. The State Department attempts to keep the matter as closely held as possible because, if it were generally known, it might 'hurt relations.' Although there have been occasional exceptions, an American who is drugged usually suffers a set back in his career, or even has his career entirely ruined."

For example, there was a U.S.–British tradition at their embassies in Moscow that the first trip taken by a new senior U.S. Army attaché would be in the company of the senior British Army attaché, and vice versa. Accordingly, in 1967, when a new British Army attaché, a brigadier, arrived in Moscow, he was escorted on his first trip by the senior U.S. Army attaché.

In Kishinev, Moldavia, the two attachés took a city tour that included a visit to a winery. After sampling the wine, they realized they had been drugged. They managed to get back to their hotel room, and managed to keep from passing out entirely. Once they were in the room, Soviets broke down the door, pulled curtains off the windows and did considerable damage to the room. Soviet photographers then took pictures. The attachés were accused of "hooliganism" and of destroying Soviet property.

The British government strongly protested the treatment of their attaché to the Soviets. However, the head of the U.S. attaché branch in the DIA (which manages the attachés) was a brigadier general with background in the military police. He took the attitude that the U.S. Army attaché was at fault for drinking wine while on a trip. The U.S. defense attaché in Moscow, an Air Force colonel, strongly protested the lack of support given to the drugged officer, and incurred the wrath of his superiors. As a result, both the defense attaché and the army attaché retired at the port upon their return to the United States.

On 21 August 1985, the State Department, with a healthy amount of righteous indignation, announced that the Soviet Union had been using a trace chemical, nitrophenylpentadienal, to follow the movements of U.S. diplomats in the Soviet Union and in other countries. The chemical would be placed where it would be picked up by an unwitting diplomat or other official—for example, on the steering wheel of a car. Traces of the chemical would then be transferred to anyone the official had contact with. The chemical, and hence the contact, could be identified by the KGB. The State Department's concern was that the chemical might be carcinogenic. Unstated was that the practice was but another way in which the Soviet intelligence forces actively employ C/B agents against foreign diplomats. Also unstated was the implication of how vulnerable any individual is under similar circumstances, especially in the event that the dust employed was something more insidious or lethal than a mere chemical tracer.

During an interview following the announcement of the Soviet use of spy dust, former U.S. Ambassador to the Soviet Union Malcolm Toon stated that the practice was not confined to official and diplomatic personnel, but to other U.S. citizens in Moscow. "I would think journalists who were in frequent contact with dissidents would be logical targets," he said. And when asked if these practices were typical Soviet behavior, he answered, "Yes, for example, we have had repeated cases ever since I became involved in Soviet affairs, going back to 1951, of beatings of our traveling personnel—primarily attachés—of druggings, of serious and intrusive harassment of personnel, then the radiation, and now this uncivilized harassment."

Another good example of this lack of U.S. sensitivity to Soviet practices, and its desire to sweep such happenings under the rug, is the case of the Ukranian seaman Miroslav Medvid. Medvid twice tried to jump from the Soviet freighter *Marshal Konev* in October 1985, while the ship was in New Orleans loading grain. When the State Department finally interviewed Medvid, it was clear he had been drugged and physically abused. In testifying before the Senate Agriculture Committee on the nature of the drugs administered, Dr. William O'Malley, an expert neurologist and psychiatrist, explained that the drugs "profoundly alter emotions and thought processes by making changes in the actual chemical composition of the human brain. For this reason, these drugs are never used in the United

States in the manner in which they were used on Mr. Medvid. . . .
The drugs exert a strong effect, diminishing the will power, and
making the patient more susceptible to conditioning. They have an
extremely potent taming effect; they even tame wild animals. In the
human, they take away aggression and combativeness, and they
produce a mental state of serenity and indifference, without simultaneously clouding consciousness." The air force psychiatrist who
interviewed Medvid for the State Department paid little attention
to the character of drugs employed or to Medvid's condition, and
returned him to the Soviets. Moreover, in a series of actions that
left several U.S. senators perplexed, State Department and National
Security Council (NSC) officials actively assisted the speedy departure of the *Marshal Konev* before the incident could be clarified and
the Soviet actions exposed to congressional scrutiny.

The deliberate murder or covert undermining of key opponents
in the West and elsewhere is one of the most important tactics utilized by the Soviet state in its quest for global supremacy. As part
of their long-term strategy, the Soviets attempt to identify and clas-
sify individuals who can be used in support of Soviet policy, and
those who are true enemies. This task is carried out by both military
and secret police agents abroad, aided by journalists and agents of
influence operating under cover in the target countries. The major
task of Yuri Bezmenov, a Novosti journalist on assignment to India
prior to his defection in 1971, was the development of a list of
exactly such people in India. He explains that there are basically
two categories of people in the Soviet classification scheme: realists
and radicals (sometimes called reactionaries). The realists understand the course of history and are perceived as being available to
assist in the attainment of Soviet goals and interests, either wittingly
or unwittingly. Such people are courted and supported, directly or
indirectly. The radicals, by contrast, are considered unsalvageable
enemies of the Soviet state and are earmarked for destruction or
neutralization. The list of these people is clearly, as he described it,
"a death list."

The methods made possible by new technology for "neutraliz-
ing" such people are especially disquieting. It is one thing to neutralize individuals by discrediting them or by provoking them to
overreact and destroy their own credibility. But today one can en-

vision even more dastardly techniques, such as covertly inducing mental impairment. An extremely useful neutralization technique is one that renders an anti-Soviet critic or rising politician ineffective without making him or her a martyr. If a leader is eliminated, another person will invariably succeed to the same leadership. However, if the leader becomes a bit mentally impaired or forgetful, or loses his or her initiative or has reduced energy, then not only the leader but the followers are effectively sabotaged.

One example will show how this can be accomplished. Among the options available is the use of radioactivity coupled with modern biochemistry to create weapons that affect personality and reasoning ability without actually killing the victim. Certain substances are now known to target selected sites of the nervous system. If such substances are radioactively labeled, they can cause permanent damage to the nervous system. If the target is a small mass of nervous tissue, only a minute amount of radiolabeled, target-specific substance is required to destroy the target. For example, should such labeling be done with a low-level beta emitter, it is highly unlikely to be detected. Yet it would be more than adequate to kill a critical number of cells, thus producing profound behavioral changes or memory loss in the victim. Although our knowledge of site-specific substances is now quite limited, this is a major area of contemporary biochemical research. Even existing techniques are more than adequate to render a problem individual "ineffective" by covertly destroying his or her short-term memory, an action that could be far more devastating than mere assassination.

Soviet and Eastern European intelligence operatives also routinely use drugs to facilitate the kidnapping and transport of individuals to Eastern bloc countries where they can be used for political and propaganda purposes, interrogated, or incarcerated. In one such case, well-known Czechoslovak émigré Bohumir Laushman was drugged by Czech intelligence officials in Austria, where he was living, and spirited back to Czechoslovakia. There he was forced, upon threats to his wife and daughter, to read a speech denouncing capitalism. By the time his speech was broadcast, both he and his family were already in jail.

In December 1975, Nicholas Shadrin, formerly Nikolay Artamonov, traveled to Vienna on a mission for the CIA. Shadrin had defected from the Soviet Union in 1959 and had been a U.S. citizen since 1965. In Vienna, a chemical substance was forcefully administered to him by Soviet KGB agents, rendering him unconscious in preparation for his quiet return to the Soviet Union. This information was received from two different sources, the second being Vitaly Yurchenko, who defected to the United States in the summer of 1985 and then subsequently redefected to the Soviet Union. His information on Shadrin, which confirmed other intelligence, was the type of data that convinced top U.S. intelligence officials that Yurchenko was a bona fide defector.

Scenario Nine: Norfolk, Virginia

Thick, dark clouds of smoke billowed from the old warehouse along Norfolk's waterfront. Firemen were working feverishly to contain the blaze and keep it from spreading to adjacent buildings. Tons of water were being poured onto the surrounding warehouses to extinguish sparks and hot ash spewing from the conflagration before they could ignite the old wooden buildings.

A panicked expression on his face, a grimy fireman, sweating heavily under his heavy protective garb despite the chill of the evening, rushed up to the Fire Chief. He had been inspecting the surrounding warehouses to make certain that none of them contained flammable materials that would add to the fire danger.

"Bad news, Chief," he gasped as snowstorm of ash swirled about them. "That old warehouse over there—," he pointed at a dilapidated gunmetal-colored two-story structure. "I think it's an illegal toxic waste storage dump. Lots of drums and containers stacked inside and some weird equipment. We're opening one of the drums now to see what's inside."

The Chief cursed and shook his head. "That's all we need." He shouted orders to one of his lieutenants to move two more pumpers into position near the suspect warehouse and intensify the streams of water being sprayed on the building. Before the lieutenant could react, a fireman staggered from the warehouse and collapsed on the pavement.

Other firemen ran to his aid but were cut down before they got close; some fell to the ground, while others, like statuary, were frozen in mid-stride.

"What the—" gasped the Chief. But the words were no sooner out of his mouth than his vision blurred and his skin began to crawl. His hands felt like they had turned to rubber and seemed to be sliding off his bones. His face was dissolving. But before he could scream, he was dead.

The President of the United States was asleep at Camp David when he was awakened by an aide who said that he had an urgent call from the National Security Advisor, Parker Knight.

"What is it now?" he grumbled as he stabbed at the flashing button on his phone.

"Yes, Parker. What is it?"

"I need to see you, sir. I have a chopper standing by to bring me up to Camp David."

"I'll be waiting for you," the President said wearily.

The President was sipping a cup of black coffee in his robe when Knight arrived, a thick sheaf of papers under one arm. They shook hands perfunctorily and Knight handed the President a three-page report on the Norfolk incident. A steward brought the National Security Advisor a cup of coffee while the President read the report.

"Unbelievable," growled the President. "This is unbelievable. You're saying that someone has been stockpiling chemical and biological weapons here, in our cities, near military facilities, and without anyone knowing? A knockout punch secreted right here under our own noses."

"That's right."

"Jesus Christ, what next." The President paused, obviously confused and upset. "How on earth could something like this happen?"

"Well, Mr. President, our borders, after all, are some of the most porous in the world. It would not be terribly difficult to ship the agents into the U.S. or even to manufacture them here. Unlike fissionable material, such agents, if properly handled, have no 'signature' or anything we can detect. They require little space, no special facilities to speak of, and only minimal personnel to activate.

We don't have all the facts yet, but it's beginning to look like some-one or some nation has set up a number of dummy chemical and toxic waste companies as a cover and used the legitimate activities of those companies to mask their real intentions."

"Why didn't we pick this up before now? Where were our in-telligence people? And who the hell's behind it?"

"Frankly, sir, at this time, all we have are suspicions. It's far too big for a terrorist operation, and too well planned for Qadaffi. Best guess now is the Soviets, either directly or through one of their sur-rogates, for example, Cuba. Certainly the Soviets are the prime sus-pect. We've known for some time that the Soviets were conducting tests in Europe designed to identify dispersal patterns of various agents depending on ambient weather conditions and things like that. They carried out a clandestine mock attack on Copenhagen in 1977, for example, which we monitored very closely, using a harm-less agent in a test similar to the ones our government conducted several decades ago in San Francisco and other cities. We believe that tests of this kind have taken place in virtually every major city in Europe. The Pentagon believes they have also tested the possi-bility of attacking key urban regions and military reservations through water supplies. We also have firm intelligence on Soviet intentions at the start of a war to activate their 'sleepers' or infiltrate spetsnaz *teams into Europe and into the U.S. to hit us in the rear with lethal or incapacitating agents—in effect crippling our ability to fight back. In Europe their plans include massive chemical and biological sabotage so as to win without destroying the industrial infrastructure. It's their answer to the neutron bomb."*

The National Security Advisor paused and lowered his eyes, staring into his coffee cup. "I suppose we should not be surprised to find that they've done the same thing here in the United States," he concluded weakly.

"And that's all we know?" The President's voice had an edge to it. "You're telling me we don't have any idea of who's doing what to us in our own country? Not a goddamn hint of it?"

"Well," replied Knight uncomfortably, "there was a Cuban de-fector who warned us that this was happening, but we turned a deaf ear. It was just too staggering to believe, and, besides, it would paint a far different picture of the Soviets than the doves in Congress and

the apologist media would have us believe. And sometimes it seems that analyses and position papers developed in our bureaucracy are governed more by the desire to have the words praised by the media than reflect the true situation. We simply have no stomach in this country for thinking the unthinkable."

The President rose and walked over to a window; hands clasped behind him, he stared out at the tranquil Maryland countryside. The dawn was just beginning to break. A gauzy mist hung in the trees and dew covered the broad lawn. Here and there the call of a songbird pierced the silence. Camp David seemed so remote from the horror they were discussing. It's a dream, isn't it, the President told himself, one of those fitful early morning dreams full of dark visions dredged up from deep within the subconscious that cause one to wake in a cold sweat. The President bit his tongue, the pain confirming that it was no dream, but instead a nightmare come true. It was the greatest crisis to face his administration; he knew it called for action—but what action?

"What now?" he asked softly, still gazing out the window.

The National Security Advisor shifted uneasily in his seat; he knew that he generally regretted quick decisions later, and he wanted time to assemble all of the facts and then turn the whole affair over in his mind for a while.

"We're checking out all of the properties owned and leased by the company leasing the warehouse, and identifying all of its officers and key employees. The FBI will run checks on their background, and hope something turns up. We've got a news blackout on the whole thing so as not to panic the public, but I don't know how long we can keep a lid on it. If it turns out to be the Soviets, then we're into a real wasps' nest. As to what we might do, . . ." he said, his voice tapering off. He rubbed the back of his neck thoughtfully. "I just don't know. But I suggest that we call a meeting of the National Security Council as soon as possible."

Neither man spoke for more than a minute, then the President turned and picked up a Bible from the corner of his desk and thumbed through the dog-eared pages.

"'My flesh is clothed with worms and clods of dust,'" he began reading, "'my skin is broken, and become loathsome.' It's a vision of the grave but I think it describes the world of living death the Soviets have planned for us."

Sabotage on the Eve of War

Another gap in U.S. political and military thinking relates to sabotage on the eve of war. The U.S. plans and programs are predicated on the assumption that warning of an impending attack will be received and that the attack will begin with the movement of many tanks, airplanes, and missiles. Without question, a war could begin in this manner. However, this is not consistent with Soviet strategy, which stresses sabotage and surprise.

Should the Soviets decide to attack, they would do so with cunning, surprise, and highly trained special operations forces (SOF), or *spetsnaz* units. The invasion of Czechoslovakia began with a meeting of Soviet and Czech leaders in a small border town to discuss mutual friendship. The conference was regarded as a great political victory for Czechoslovakia. When interviewed upon his return to Prague, the leader of the Czech Catholic Party related that Comrade Brezhnev, with tears in his eyes, had complained about Western "propaganda" purporting that the Soviet Union was preparing to invade Czechoslovakia. "How can people believe that?" Brezhnev reportedly asked. "We are your best friends and brothers." Two months later, Soviet special forces seized government and military communications centers, most key decisionmakers, and the main airport. Special propaganda troops took over major radio stations. Airborne reinforcements landed at the airport and extended their control over the country. Subsequently the attack by tanks and infantry began. The same basic pattern of events preceded the invasion of Afghanistan.

The Soviets believe that it makes little sense to attack a forewarned, well-prepared enemy. Rather, with the use of special operations forces, the enemy first should be covertly attacked to undermine its ability to respond. Deception and sabotage are to be used to confuse and wound the opponent prior to the main attack. The contrasting U.S. view of special operations is important because it differs so dramatically from the Soviet perspective, which emphasizes the use of chemical, toxin, and biological weapons in sabotage operations.

In the U.S. military establishment, special operations forces are not only deemphasized, they are too often even denigrated. In 1985, special operations forces received only twenty-five cents out of every hundred dollars in the Pentagon budget. There has been some improvement in subsequent budgets, but the figure is still far too low. Traditionally special operations forces have been opposed by many in the military as elitist, not to mention the fact that special operations forces do not translate into large dollars, manpower requirements, big hardware items, and lots of generals and admirals. Rather, special operations forces stress ingenuity and sophistication, high-leverage, low-profile operations, and considerable discipline, all of which may explain their lack of popularity. There has been far too little attention given by the U.S. military to many of the traditional capabilities emphasized by special operations forces, especially sabotage and behind-the-lines operations.

By contrast, sabotage is a major element of Soviet strategy. Warsaw Pact defectors (who had access to plans and came from sabotage units) have stated that a war with NATO or the United States would begin with sabotage operations and that C/B weapons would be employed. All important targets are to be attacked in different ways, the first of which generally is sabotage. The Soviets reportedly plan to deploy several hundred *spetsnaz* units against European targets. The number assigned for action in the United States might well be comparable, if not greater in number.

Both the KGB and the GRU have sabotage departments. (This pattern is repeated throughout the Soviet Union's client states.) The work is normally divided up. The KGB generally takes action against political and civilian targets. A good example of a political target is the former president of Afghanistan, Hafizullah Amin, who was assassinated just prior to the Soviet invasion. Originally, Amin was to have been poisoned by a KGB agent, one of Amin's cooks.

The GRU-trained officers, attached to military commands and high-level staff organizations, handle military, military–industrial and military–economic targets. Both the KGB and GRU run training facilities. Recruits of all nationalities, including Americans, are trained at these centers. Basic training for non-Soviets takes place in many communist countries; but, advanced training for those that excel both substantively and ideologically is conducted exclusively within the Soviet Union. There are reports of special camps where trained personnel live for extended periods of time and where only the language, customs, and money of the targeted country are used.

Sabotage against the Soviets' enemies is carefully organized and uses Soviet and surrogate sabotage agents, both in-place and inserted. Many agents are already in the targeted countries, as are most of the required weapons and supplies. According to Soviet doctrine, additional *spetsnaz* troops are to be inserted into adversary nations before the conflict begins. Given the ease of penetrating U.S. borders, there would be little problem for an enemy to bring explosives and large quantities of C/B agents into the United States (or even into other NATO countries). Indeed, one communist defector has alleged that the Soviets have already prepositioned C/B agents east of the Mississippi River, although this cannot be verified.

Sabotage groups may be as small as one or two individuals who are entrusted with very specific tasks (such as assassinations), or as large as a thousand team members for an attack on a major complex. The normal group, however, contains five or six members. Control is exercised through Soviet agents in-place, using Soviets officers as leaders whenever possible. In each country, there are several independent GRU and KGB nets to preserve security.

In periods of crisis, when war is considered imminent, preparations are carried to the point where operations can be put into action at a moment's notice.

Targets are not necessarily located in proximity to the responsible agent's peacetime base of operations. To guard against discovery and arrest during crisis preparations, agents often are positioned in countries or regions quite removed from their designated targets. Thus, agent groups located in Sweden might be targeted against West Germany, Belgium, and Great Britain, as well as against the host country.

Sabotage operations will be directed at military units and facilities, political or administration elements, military–industrial facilities, and specific individuals. In the broadest sense, the objective of such sabotage will be to cripple the enemy's ability to mobilize and go to war. Sabotage may take place at the onset of hostilities or perhaps days, weeks, or even months earlier.

In Soviet terminology, the euphemisms *diversionary, special,* or *spetsnaz* operations are used to refer to sabotage. A particularly good description, where the subject is called "special reconnaissance," is presented in the current *Soviet Military Encyclopedia.* Special reconnaissance is "carried out to subvert the political, economic, military, and moral potential of a probable or actual enemy.

The primary missions of special reconnaissance are: acquiring intelligence on major economic and military installations and either destroying them or putting them out of action; organizing sabotage and acts of subversion and terrorism; carrying out punitive operations against patriotic forces; conducting hostile propaganda; forming and training insurgent detachments, etc." Such operations are to be "conducted by the forces of covert intelligence and special purpose troops." Among the special weapons listed for use in special reconnaissance are "biological weapons, narcotics, and poisons."

Soviet and Eastern European literature exhibits a keen awareness of the potentials of high-tech C/B agents in sabotage and special operations. A particularly good example is contained in a 1967 East German military chemistry manual in which "psychotoxins are credited with strategic importance as diversion and sabotage poisons." Using only relatively small amounts, the text points out, "great effects can be achieved in the interior, if the actions are well planned. By poisoning water-supply facilities and the like, large portions of the population can be made incapable of action for a certain period of time. Breakdowns in sensitive production areas, anxiety, uncertainty, and unpredictable actions would be the results."

The East German text also points out that psychotoxins have special advantages not shared by other chemical warfare agents. Incapacity is brought about "by extremely slight doses or concentrations too small to be detected with conventional methods of detection." Moreover, the agents are described as "colorless, odorless, and tasteless. They can be used both as combat chemical agents and as sabotage poisons for the poisoning of water, foodstuffs, and luxuries. The compounds chosen are extremely stable in the atmosphere and even in water."

A 1977 East German text describes toxins that are ten million times more toxic than the nerve agent soman. They are said, moreover, to be simple to produce "in large amounts, using continuous processes," a specific reference to the application of biotechnology to C/B warfare. In a similar manner, the *Soviet Military Encyclopedia* refers to neurotropic toxins as "the most toxic chemical substances of all known toxic agents," and explains that these agents can be used as an aerosol or in solid or liquid state, and that "they can also be used for sabotage purposes."

Such references are repeated many times in discussions of biological warfare in the *Soviet Military Encyclopedia*. Biological weapons are said to be highly effective in view of (1) the small doses required; (2) the possibility of concealed employment over a large area: (3) the difficulty of detection; (4) the selectivity available (only on humans, on given types of animals, etc.); (5) the strong psychological pressure; (6) the amount deployed; (7) the difficulty of biological protection of troops and population; and (8) the liquidation of their effects.

When sabotage takes place well in advance of hostilities, considerable value is placed on having agents or substances that are both hard to detect and difficult to identify. The notion of covertness and clandestine employment permeates the Soviet discussions of biochem sabotage. Obviously, form the saboteur's point of view, it is generally best to have an event appear to be a natural phenomenon. However, the simple inability of the victimized party to explain with assurance what has happened or to place the blame where it belongs will be sufficient to achieve the saboteur's purpose.

The development of an agent that can survive in a chlorinated water supply would have a great deal of utility to a saboteur in view of the ease and covertness of delivery. One can envision a range of acceptable options, from the gradual poisoning of a water supply to introducing agents with rapid but short-duration effects. Poisoning or contaminating the water supplies of important political administration regions have been a reported Soviet objective. There is reason to believe that Cuba may have been assigned such sabotage missions in the United States on the eve of war or in the event of a major national crisis. Many important military and political installations are critically dependent on water supplies from external sources that are easily accessible to trained saboteurs. There is considerable evidence that Soviet-sponsored *spetsnaz* units have regularly run mock assaults on sabotage targets in Western Europe and in the United States. Special trace elements (some perhaps radioactively labeled) can be used well in advance of actual hostilities to covertly test the efficiency with which water supply systems can be contaminated.

There are intelligence reports that new organisms with military applications have been developed in the Soviet Union, but not necessarily manufactured. When war is viewed as inevitable, small quantities of the organisms can be smuggled into target countries where they are grown into the required quantities in a few days by trained agents. The 1984 U.S. presidential report on Soviet noncompliance with arms control treaties confirms that fast-growing agents are under development by the Soviets using genetic engineering techniques.

The most challenging Soviet sabotage targets during a crisis are closed facilities, both military and political. These include the White House; presidential and successor relocation facilities; military command and control centers such as NORAD, Fort Ritchie, and Omaha; air bases; Minuteman wing control centers and launch facilities; and, especially, submarines. During a crisis, such facilities become semisealed environments where no one enters or leaves without high-priority need. The only exceptions are the provision of routine services including food delivery, mail, cleaning, and so forth. In-place agents would be an obvious enemy asset. On the other hand, they may be considered undependable because in such a crisis a prudent planner assumes that all suspected agents will be arrested and detained. The question remains, how can such facilities be sabotaged? The time available to the saboteur may be as short as a few days or weeks, but most likely will be measured in months. In most cases, something like fifty people or less work closely together in a closed area for an extended period of time, and disabling only a few of them would be inadequate. Notwithstanding the apparent difficulties, many modern biochem possibilities are available. Extremely potent chemicals or devilishly clever organisms can be introduced into such facilities through the food, drink, clothing, mail, or people who enter the facility. An individual who works in the facility, an enemy "sleeper" or deep cover agent, can with little difficulty hide on his or her person or belongings an ample quantity of an agent to disable several thousand individuals or to contaminate the largest such facility.

Now, and for the foreseeable future, it is inconceivable to most defense analysts that the United States will strike first in a general war situation, independent of Soviet actions. Though Soviet planners assume the enemy is prudent and recognizes the value of striking first, they have ample reason to doubt that the United States will ever start such a war. Certainly, the focus of their strategic intelligence is to detect any U.S. decision to strike first. At the same time, Soviet strategy calls for deceptive actions designed to mislead the West into lowering its guard while the Soviets covertly go to maximum readiness in advance of a first strike. This process could take place over several days, or even several months, allowing sufficient time to implement carefully planned sabotage operations throughout the West. As an opening salvo, the Soviets might well initiate a massive covert C/B war that would confuse the leadership of the Western alliance and distract their attention away from even more critical events. In the process, the Soviets could effectively disable U.S. forces and disrupt the civilian population, making it impossible for the United States to go to war, except as an act of extreme desperation.

As an indication of the apparent ease with which this type of sabotage could be conducted, the Soviets are known to routinely position agents in the vicinity of many U.S. and NATO military installations. For example, these agents operate fast-food stores, shoe repair services, dry cleaning establishments, and gas stations. Most of the food and water used on military and political installations comes from off base and is easily accessed by trained agents. Further, as will be described later, the Soviets (through their Eastern bloc surrogates and Cuba) have built up a worldwide network of agents for the distribution of hashish and narcotics into the military and society that, upon command, could easily be laced with special substances. This, in turn, would cause erratic behavior on the part of literally hundreds of thousands or millions of people. If the substance were lethal, this could result in a epidemic of drug-related deaths and overdoses that would overwhelm big-city health-care systems.

The severity of this threat to the United States has intensified as a result of the self-destruction of the U.S. internal security capabilities that took place during the period 1973–76. The threat is especially grim when coupled with the concomitant flood of tens of thousands of émigrés and refugees from communist-dominated regions during the 1970s and 1980s. Most are legitimate refugees, but intelligence sources indicate that large numbers of enemy agents or sleepers have infiltrated into the United States along with the refugee population. These sleepers would be activated as needed to carry out intelligence or sabotage missions against targets in this country. As an indication of the diminished U.S. capability to monitor such potential saboteurs, the number of cases of "subversives and extremists" under investigation by the FBI dropped from fifty-five thousand in 1974, to roughly twenty thousand by the summer of 1975, to slightly over one hundred in 1977, to seventeen in 1982. All this helps explain why Arnaud de Borchgrave testified before Congress in 1983 that the KGB and its subsidiary, the Cuban *Dirección General de Inteligencia* (DGI), operate freely in the United States, and that "the DGI regards internal security in the U.S. as a joke." Some improvement has been evidenced under the Reagan administration, but efforts are still inadequate. Moreover, even under the best of circumstances, it will take years, perhaps even a generation, to restore and revitalize U.S. internal security capabilities.

Scenario Ten: California

With less than two weeks to go before the rich California primary, the fight over the nomination as the party standard-bearer had come down to two serious candidates: Governor Arthur O'Connor and Senator Jake Billings. O'Connor had begun to fade under Senator Billings's relentless hammering. Billings had exposed O'Connor not only as thin on the issues but as less than honest about the nature and extent of his financial dealings. Billings was one of the Senate's brightest stars, a brilliant neoconservative from the West who had punched all the right tickets: Harvard, Rhodes scholar, Vietnam combat veteran, professional athlete, college president. Few had given him much chance when he had announced his candidacy the previous year, but as the more conventional and better-known hopefuls failed to catch on and began falling by the wayside, Billings picked up money and momentum, and gradually turned skeptics into believers. Now he was poised on the threshold of winning his party's nomination for the highest office in the land, and the pundits were already casting him as the odds-on favorite in the November general election.

In the Kremlin, the Soviet leadership watched Billings's rise with trepidation. An archfoe of the Soviet Union and Senate champion of support for anti-Soviet insurgent movements, Billings was viewed as dangerous and unpredictable, the kind of man who would contest Moscow for every square inch of territory and every last measure of global influence. The incumbent president, by contrast, while a weak and uninspiring leader, had advanced a conciliatory policy toward the Soviet Union characterized by vacillation and impotence in the face of Soviet transgressions. As a result, he was regarded by the Soviet leadership as the kind of man they could do business with, an establishment figure with a well-known track record.

With the imminent prospect of Senator Billings wrapping up the nomination, the six most powerful men in the Kremlin, the Defense Council, had been called together in an emergency session by the General Secretary to review the KGB analysis of the candidates and discuss how the U.S. election would potentially affect the Soviet Union and its national interests. One by one, each individual at the table expressed his apprehensions concerning Billings, and all agreed with Marshal Kuznetsov that a Billings victory in November could set the world revolutionary movement back in Africa, Latin America, and the Middle East.

"If I read your sentiments correctly, comrades," summarized the General Secretary peering over the top of his reading glasses, "We all agree that something must be done, and that extraordinary measures may even be called for."

No dissent was voiced.

"In view of the urgency of the problem," continued the General Secretary, "I would like to turn the meeting over to Comrade Voloshin, who is prepared to present us with a most interesting proposal that may offer a way out of our current dilemma." He put down his pen and folded his hands in front of him.

Yuri Voloshin was chief of the KGB, and the other members of the Defense Council turned to him expectantly, each wondering how much Voloshin knew about his personal operations. A small taciturn man, his eyes concealed behind blue-tinted spectacles, his mannerisms stiff and restrained, Voloshin cleared his throat and glanced around the table unemotionally, with a face more suggestive of waiting for a bus than plotting the future of the Western world.

"Since it is our collective judgment," he began, stressing the word "collective," "that this man Billings represents, very possibly,

an intolerable threat to our long-term interests, then perhaps we should ensure that he never is in a position to do real harm to us."

"Fine idea," Marshal Kuznetsov mumbled sarcastically, "But how? We decided last week that the situation was not appropriate for affecting the imperialists' elections as Comrade Surov so successfully did back in 1964. And as dangerous as this fellow seems, his elimination would be too risky. Better to watch carefully and turn him after the election as we have done so successfully in the past. After all, the U.S. President doesn't make policy, he only thinks he does."

"Ah, my dear Kuznetsov," replied Voloshin softly, a hint of reproach in his voice. "What we have in mind is infinitely more subtle than anything we have discussed before." The KGB chief cleared his throat once again and let his words sink in. "We have it in our power to make Mr. Billings, what the Americans might say, 'tune in, turn on, and drop out.' Comrades, we will help Billings self-destruct." He frowned at Marshal Kuznetsov, with the disdain of a schoolmaster chastising a bumbling schoolboy.

"Pray continue, comrade," the Prime Minister urged, speaking for all the others, with only transparently suppressed excitement in this voice.

"It is simple, comrades," continued Voloshin. "We have a 'sleeper' in Senator Billings's household, a housekeeper who claims to be from the Dominican Republic, but who, in reality, is a Cuban intelligence officer. Among her responsibilities is the duty of preparing a light breakfast for the Senator—"

"You're suggesting we poison him?" interrupted Kuznetsov. "Remember Afghanistan and Algeria? You seriously think we can get away with it?"

Voloshin waited for Kuznetsov to finish, then resumed in a flat, cold voice that made even the General Secretary shiver inwardly. "Our scientists have developed a remarkable substance, a combination of radiochemistry and genetic engineering, which is capable of producing profound behavioral changes in people. A low-power beta emitter is attached to a special, small molecule that has a strong affinity for certain cells in the brain. The molecule attaches to and then kills these cells, and produces disorientation, memory loss, confusion, and a reduced attention span. It is undetectable. Only something on the order of a picogram, which is a millionth of a millionth of a gram, is necessary to induce the changes I'm talking about. The agent on Senator Billings's household staff could easily slip such a minute amount into his morning coffee or his scrambled eggs without anyone being the wiser. And, if the housekeeper is denied the opportunity, we have at least three other backup systems for administering the substance." Voloshin's voice dropped to a whisper. He made a clutching motion with his hand, drawing the eyes of all council members to the imaginary figure in his grasp. "In short, comrades, we can neutralize Billings before he causes us any real discomfort. The method I propose is cheap, effective, and, above all, virtually foolproof. It is something we have been saving for a special occasion." Voloshin's jaw snapped shut with an audible click and he settled back into his chair, his dark suit blending into the upholstery. Despite his obvious triumph, his expression remained set, unemotional. Only his close friend and long-time antagonist at the State Planning Commission, Vasily Rumsov, could detect the beginnings of a slight smile.

"Then it is unanimous?" asked the General Secretary, surveying the assembled group.

As expected, Senator Billings won the California primary and locked up his party's nomination for the presidency. However, upon returning from a short vacation, he appeared somewhat listless and easily distracted. His responses to questions and interviews were careless and often contradictory. He seemed to have lost his talent for the quick and humorous retort. His campaign appearances were also flat and unimpressive. In the first of two nationally televised debates with the incumbent, he stumbled over questions that only a short time earlier would have been child's play, and even the most generous political commentators rated the matchup a draw. Aides attributed his weak performance to "exhaustion" and announced they were going to cut back on Billings's campaign schedule. However, that didn't seem to help; the second debate came and went without any noticeable improvement in the challenger's performance. Many of those who had greeted Billings's decision to seek the Presidency with so much excitement and expectation began to reassess their original impression. Far from being a man of extraordinary depth and perception, in the glare of television lights and incessant scrutiny, he seemed to be positively ordinary.

Despite Billings's disappointing performance in the campaign, the election was still close, owing more to the weakness of the incumbent than to the strength of the challenger. Nevertheless, the incumbent managed to capture two critical swing states in the early morning hours of 7 November, which gave him three more electoral votes than necessary. That same evening, in the Kremlin, members of the Soviet Defense Council began assembling for another emergency session that had been called three hours earlier to review certain recent operations. In light of their favorable outcome, they were to decide on a more elaborate KGB plan to gradually educate the anti-Soviet capitalists who continued to obstruct social progress and interfere with the natural laws of history.

Chemical War and Mind Control

In 1977, the World Psychiatric Association (WPA) condemned the Soviet Union for using psychiatric diagnosis and treatment to punish political dissidents. For years the Soviets had been using neuroleptic and experimental drugs and various forms of shock therapy on dissidents and political prisoners. The treatments were intended to change the dissidents' attitudes and thinking both by chemically attacking their brains and by inducing psychological trauma. The practices amounted to nothing less than a combination of lobotomies and torture using chemicals and electricity. The practices were so widespread throughout the Soviet Union, and so repugnant to free-world scientists, that the WPA took the highly unusual step of publicly rebuking the Soviets.

Rather than modify any of their practices, the Soviet response was to attack the WPA as a tool of Western imperialism. Meanwhile, reports on the practices continued to leak out of the Soviet Union. Many complaints were filed with the WPA, which forwarded them to the Soviet member society. With few exceptions, Soviet psychiatrists have refused to respond. By 1982. it was clear that the Soviet Union was not about to change. It was equally clear that such behavior were well outside the range of tolerable medical practices as viewed by the membership of the WPA. The movement to censure the Soviets gathered momentum, and by February 1983, it appeared likely that the Soviets would be suspended or expelled from the WPA at the May meeting. The Soviet response again was to attack the WPA and, in anticipation of the disciplinary action, the Soviet All-Union Society of Psychiatrists and Neuropathologists withdrew its membership in the WPA.

In the attack on Soviet psychiatric practices, attention was focused on the so-called punitive medicine practiced in the Soviet Union. Unfortunately, little was said of what might be a more fundamental reason behind these medical practices: the underlying assumption of Soviet ideology, whereby the spiritual side of human nature is denied, individual behavior is determined by the biochemical processes, and deviation from that which is expected or demanded is subject to "correction." Punishment and reward are ingrained in the Soviet approach to determining the behavior of individuals, and so is the ability to manipulate behavior through chemicals. Dissidents are considered sick. Doctors in Soviet mental hospitals have the task of reinforcing the notion that dissidents are mentally ill. In this connection, doctors administer drugs to political dissidents that impede the latter's judgment, thinking, and memory, and eventually produce permanent mental derangement.

Research and development of drugs designed to achieve various forms of mind control is a Soviet priority. The Soviets believe in the value and potential of this effort, and have expended considerable resources to achieve results. This is an activity that goes hand-in-hand with their psychological theories and, more importantly, with their ideology. As early as 1953, KGB chief Beria told a U.S. research physician that he had eight neuropharmacologists on his staff. (This was coincident with the appearance and successful use of the first neuroleptic drug, chlorpromazine.) The staff's activities expanded, as did the field of neuropsychopharmacology. All this slowly became public knowledge as refugees from the Gulag of psychoprisons and mental institutions made their way to the West, or smuggled out first-hand accounts of their ordeals. (Such institutions received expanded emphasis after Yuri Andropov took over the KGB in 1967.)

The development of drugs for large-scale mind control as a natural component of Soviet biochem R&D is undoubtedly a major Soviet objective. As pointed out in a 1967 East German text, the field of psychotoxins "is by no means a closed subject; rather it is the beginning of a development that is directed toward the complete influence and control over human consciousness." Almost identical comments are present in papers prepared for a "disarmament" conference of scientists that was held in East Berlin in 1971: "Psychotoxins are weapons directed against the further existence of an independently thinking and acting society."

The significance of the entire spectrum of political- and intelligence-related warfare research lies in its relationship to Marxist-Leninist ideology and the inner workings of the Soviet state. The heart of the Soviet state philosophy and organization is total centralized control and unity of thought—Marxist-Leninist thought. Only those discussions or arguments that are officially sanctioned are tolerated. Any dissent or departure from the party position is undertaken by an individual at the risk of being branded an enemy of the state. The implications of such action are expulsion from the party (if the perpetrator is a party member), imprisonment in a labor camp to enable the guilty to work off their sins, or assignment to appropriate mental institution or hospital for treatment. There are no individual rights, safeguards, or ethical standards in the Soviet Union as those words are understood in the West.

The Soviet leadership (that is, the party hierarchy) has approached its "mission" with the dedication and long-term perspective of a never-ending crusade. As explained by Dr. John Dziak, a specialist on Soviet political and intelligence operations, the best way to view the Soviet state apparatus is as a massive counterintelligence apparatus dedicated to root out and destroy all enemies of the party: people, ideas, organizations, and nations. The ability to change the minds of the opposition with drugs is a capability that is not realizable in any sense of the word (that is, there is no pro-Soviet pill). However, the willingness to frighten, intimidate, drug into senselessness, pacify, cripple, or kill is real—and has been widely exploited by the Soviets against all forms of opposition.

One of the by-products of modern biochemical technology is the effectiveness and efficiency with which all of the above can be practiced, and practiced covertly. This is the clear warning contained in a number of writings of Eastern European C/B scientists.

These objectives and others—for example, controlling the "psychic state" of populations, undermining morale, destroying willpower, and separating man from the realities of his environment—are explicitly stated in Soviet military literature and also can be inferred from research interests as reflected in Soviet scientific writings since the mid-1970s.

The use of drugs for political purposes is certainly not limited to internal Soviet practices. Diplomats, attachés, foreign technicians, émigrés and defectors, politicians in foreign countries, and Western society in general have been targets, and this intelligence is well-documented. The potential for further development of drugs that can be administered covertly and used to influence behavior and states of mind becomes especially ominous in light of present Soviet practices and Moscow's strategy of infiltrating and sabotaging hostile organizations in foreign countries. The tools that are being developed for the treatment of mental illness and for mind control can enable an intelligence agent or small group of agents who have penetrated a target organization or country (1) to covertly assassinate or discredit an individual or group of individuals; (2) to discredit or neutralize whole organizations; (3) to disturb or distort decisionmakers' mental processes; and (4) to put even a region or entire nation to "sleep."

The Soviet strategy of infiltration and sabotage has been pursued since the Communist International was formed shortly after Lenin seized control of Russia. All national and important public and private organizations within each nation are to be targeted. The Soviet goal is to take control of important societal organizations, turn them to the service of the Soviet cause, disrupt the targeted society, and then take over and impose a dictatorship of the proletariat. People who stand in the way are to be overcome or otherwise eliminated. What better way than with the application of sophisticated chemicals or organisms designed to debilitate the opposition?

It is frightening to consider the ease with which this can be accomplished, given the vast array of scientific techniques recently developed to treat mental illness. Many more possibilities will emerge as methods of controlling various diseases are developed. Indeed, the mere study of diseases with profound mental side effects may be a very useful approach. Consider, for example, one of the more bizarre diseases, encephalitis lethargica, also known as sleeping sickness. This disease struck several million people in Europe and the United States after World War I. Isolating the responsible proteins has been the cornerstone of understanding diseases (such as this) that affect the central nervous system. Once the protein is isolated, the responsible gene can then be produced. The gene can be incorporated into an otherwise harmless organism, which can then be covertly introduced into the unsuspecting victim.

One of the advantages the Soviets have in pursuing such research is an unlimited supply of human guinea pigs. The Soviet practice of using humans for such experiments has been well documented in the Hirsch report, which was compiled following World War II. Additional confirmation of this despicable yet routine Soviet practice has come from 1970s high level defectors and émigrés. They have reported that the use of humans in experiments is not limited to prisoners and dissidents, but even extends to citizens who are used without their knowledge in chemical warfare research.

Testifying before Congress in 1976, Luba Markish described how chemicals were administered to her, without her knowledge at the time, while she was a student at Moscow State University. A émigré chemical engineer, Professor David Azbel, confirmed her statements and recited his personal direct knowledge of chemical experiments against whole rural village communities. According to Azbel, there was a limit to the utility of prisoners and unsuspecting rural villagers for C/B warfare experiments. Prisoners were inadequate research subjects because of their generally weakened physical condition; rural villagers were unsatisfactory because they were not located near the hospitals where C/B warfare research was conducted. To transport them to the hospitals would have entailed an unacceptable security risk. It was not unusual, therefore, to select university students as unwitting volunteers. (A wider variety of experimental biochem agents could be tested on them without concern over resultant deaths or mental incapacities. The results were naturally explainable as "student's accidents.") Azbel described priority research interests that concentrated "on poison gases that act on the brain and the nervous system."

Within the Marxist-Leninist code that governs Soviet behavior, there are no laws or morals as those terms are understood in the West. Laws and morals are derived to support the world socialist movement, and whatever advances that movement is not only legal and moral, it is right and to be employed. This is the philosophy that needs to be clearly recognized in assessing the alarming and far-reaching implications of high-tech biological warfare.

4
Chemical War with Drugs and Narcotics

The Growing Problem

America is confronted with an enormous illegal drug and narcotics problem. "The incidence of substance abuse in 1986 is a national crisis that is totally out of hand. We have never seen the level of abuse that exists today," explains Dr. Joseph Troiani, director of alcohol and drug abuse for Loretto Hospital in Chicago and president of the Chicago Alcohol and Drug Abuse Commission.

Fueling increased public concern, drug and narcotics use has passed the $100-billion-per-year level. It is responsible for escalating health expenses and absenteeism that may exceed $50 billion per year. Use doubled between 1980 and 1985 and spread to the middle-class and white-collar workers. New York City has had over a 100 percent increase in drug-related deaths. Drugs and narcotics are recognized as the single major cause of violent crime. In 1986, two famous athletes were cut down in their prime.

Congress deserves much of the credit today for recognizing the nature of the drug and narcotics problem and increasing its visibility. In particular, the House Select Committee on Narcotics Abuse and Control under Charles B. Rangel and the Senate Labor and Human Resources Committee's Subcommittee on Drugs and Alcoholism under Paula Hawkins have held numerous hearings that have served to expose the problem to public scrutiny. Their findings are discouraging and disconcerting.

Most discouraging has been their revelation of the extent and growth of the problem in the United States, notwithstanding increased efforts by the responsible government agencies to combat the trafficking. As stated by the House Select Committee in 1984, "Not only have we failed to progress or hold a status quo, we have retrogressed enormously during the past five years."

The congressional hearings have also convincingly verified that the organizations behind the flow of narcotics into the United States are not the Mafia or organized crime or the many unprincipled individuals from all walks of life. Drug and narcotics trafficking is chiefly an operation run by governments hostile to the United States and by various terrorist and revolutionary war forces. In nearly all cases, these nations and sub-national organizations are Soviet satellites or pro-Soviet organizations.

The drug and narcotics trafficking, amply serious in its own regard, is made doubly so by virtue of its marriage to international terrorism. These two despicable activities have merged since the mid-1970s, with the terrorists providing protection to the traffickers and the traffickers financing terrorist activities. The merger of the two has become so complete in all regions of the globe that the two groups are becoming indistinguishable. The descriptive name coined to reflect the new couplet is *narcoterrorism*. The common objective of both the terrorists and the narcotics traffickers is to bring down political order.

That the chief objective of narcotics trafficking is political is perhaps the most shocking revelation of the Rangel and Hawkins committee investigations. Profit is definitely a major motivation. Money provides the grease: it corrupts the nonideologically motivated individual participants; it makes the operation self-financing; and it provides an important source of currency for the participating nations. But money is not the essential reason for the trafficking. That reason, as explained by high-ranking officials from the involved countries, is to destroy the social fabric of the Western societies. The fundamental basis of the drug and narcotics trafficking into the United States—and into Britain, Ireland, Italy, and so forth—is political warfare.

Probably no better description of the trafficking nations' motivation exists than that provided by Antonio Farach, former minister-counselor, in the Nicaraguan Embassies in Venezuela and Honduras. He explained that in discussing their narcotics trafficking operation, high ranking Nicaraguan officials used two moral and political justifications: "In the first place, drugs did not remain in Nicaragua. The drugs were destined for the United States. Our youth would not be harmed, but rather the youth of the United States, the youth of our enemies. Therefore the drugs were used as a political weapon because in that way we were delivering a blow to our principal enemy. . . . Second, in addition to a political weapon against the United States, the drug trafficking produced a very good economic benefit which we needed for our revolution. Again, in a few words, we wanted to provide food to our people with the suffering and death of the youth of the United States."

In reality, drug and narcotics trafficking is the most heinous form of chemical warfare that is being waged, and waged unilaterally, today. Unquestionably, there are right-wing terrorists involved, and many of the participants are respectable citizens of all countries, but they are but a small part of the problem. The chief component of the drug and narcotics trafficking, the main reason efforts to combat it have been so unsuccessful, is that it is in reality a serious covert war being conducted deliberately by communist nations, parties, and terrorists against the West.

This basis of the drug problem is the most important message that has surfaced during the congressional investigations, but neither it nor its implications (as with other aspects of C/B warfare) have yet to attract much attention. The crime is so enormous that it is hard to imagine that nations (not just individuals) are not only deliberately involved, but, indeed, are directly responsible. Attention has been severely limited because the trafficking operations are under the control and direction of foreign nations (and usually directed by the intelligence departments of those nations). Thus, much of the data needed to combat the drug problem lies in the domain of U.S. intelligence, not with the narcotics divisions of the State and Justice Departments or the U.S. Customs Service. Unfortunately, testimony by U.S. intelligence community personnel has been conspicuously absent from the congressional hearings.

The roles played by the Soviet Union and the People's Republic of China are also ignored in the congressional hearings and in the public perception of the problem. Except for occasional references, neither nation has received serious attention in the congressional hearings or in the media. This would seem to be a gap in our comprehension of the problem. The Soviet Union is known to exercise close control over the activities of its satellites, especially the operations of their intelligence departments, which is where the direction of the narcotics and terrorist activities emanates. In the case of China, its current role is less certain. However, the current use of narcotics and drugs against the United States in war originated with China, and was a major weapon utilized by China against U.S. military forces during the Vietnam War.

Illegal drugs and narcotics have been a steadily escalating problem since the late 1940s. They are undermining the social fabric of the United States, and other nations as well, and contributing to instabilities and vulnerabilities within the military forces. In brief, the drug and narcotics trafficking is a serious national security problem. It is a modern-day form of chemical warfare. Until this fact is recognized, further efforts to combat the problem are destined to be as ineffective as have been efforts over the past thirty-five years.

The Rise of Communist Narcotics Trafficking

The communist trafficking operation began shortly after World War II, when China and North Korea started smuggling heroin into Japan as a weapon directed against the Japanese and U.S. military forces. The Criminal Investigation Division of the American Forces in Japan began an investigation of illegal opium and heroin in 1949, which led to the capture of 3,878 kilograms of pure heroin in packages marked "Duro-Well Pharmaceutical Laboratory, Lions Globe Brand, Luck Street, Tientsin."

This is also the time that heroin addiction suddenly increased in the United States. Heroin addiction had almost disappeared during World War II. Soon thereafter, however, the problem began to increase, with a marked rise occurring in the late 1940s and early 1950s. The U.S. Bureau of Narcotics traced the origins of the supply increase and determined that the source was the People's Republic of China. In partial confirmation of this, the Bureau of Narcotics seized large shipments of contraband Chinese heroin in New York and San Francisco harbors in 1952. Harry Anslinger, the head of the U.S. Bureau of Narcotics, stated that the United States knew both the names and location of those in China who were responsible for the narcotics smuggling. "The Mafia," he said in response to press reports, "was not the biggest drug dealer. This was a false impression. By far the biggest drug dealer was Peking."

China's involvement in heroin, opium, and morphine trafficking into Japan and the United States was confirmed by several of the dealers apprehended at the time and by detailed reports from undercover treasury agents in Hong Kong. Of more interest, however, was the testimony of a high-level Chinese communist party functionary who defected in 1959. He described a secret meeting in Peking in 1952 attended by, among others, officials of the Chinese Export Ministry, Finance Ministry, and National Planning Commission. The subject of the meeting was how to increase the national income by exporting narcotics. China's trade policies were unhampered by Western moral compunctions. To the contrary, they viewed the operation as merely another phase in the opium wars, for which Mao Tse-tung held the British and Americans responsible.

Taipei and Moscow have both accused China of trafficking and have, independently, estimated China's income in 1952 at $70 million, which might roughly correspond to a street value of $7 billion. By 1964, following an expansion of China's production capability as part of the "Great Leap Forward" in 1958–60, the estimated trade value of China's trafficking had grown to $500 million. Perhaps coincidently, the second major post–World War II increase in U.S. heroin addiction was during the late 1950s and early 1960s— in almost perfect synchronization with the increase in the supply of Chinese heroin achieved during the Great Leap Forward.

China also started the practice of using heroin as a weapon against U.S. fighting forces. During the Korean War, China and North Korea supplied high-quality, low-cost heroin for use by U.S. troops. The narcotics were marketed in the immediate vicinity of U.S. military bases throughout the peninsula. These facts were determined by U.S. Army intelligence and subsequently have been confirmed by Jan Sejna, who in the mid-1950s read a classified Soviet analysis of the Chinese use of narcotics against U.S. military forces.

The Soviet study was a joint effort by Soviet, Czechoslovak, and North Korean doctors to determine the physical and mental effect of the narcotics on combat soldiers. The doctors conducted autopsies on the bodies of U.S. and South Korean soldiers. The findings were most surprising: 22 percent of the U.S. soldiers were determined to have had "mini-heart attacks," as the Soviets called them. Soviet intelligence estimated that 60 percent of the U.S. servicemen had tried drugs by the end of the war. In contrast, only 2 percent of the South Korean soldiers were found to have had heart damage. Additionally, the South Korean use of drugs was half that of the U.S. soldiers (30 percent). In contrast to the U.S. soldiers' habits (which were oriented to the hard drugs), the Koreans were mainly smokers of marijuana and, to a lesser extent, opium. The Soviets were impressed by these results, which showed that the narcotics trafficking not only provided results of tactical value, but had significant long-range strategic implications. This Soviet use of the dead enemy soldiers, distasteful as it must seem to most Americans, is not an isolated incident. In the early 1980s in the war in Afghanistan, the refugees told of Soviets, often wearing chemical warfare protective garb, entering combat areas shortly after the areas had been subjected to attack with chemicals or toxins, removing dead bodies, and in some cases, extracting specific organs and leaving the mutilated bodies to be disposed of by the Soviet security forces that arrived shortly thereafter. In light of the Soviet study of the U.S. and South Korean corpses, the Afghanistan stories become much more believable. The Soviets were conducting experiments with new C/B agents and were merely collecting data for use in assessing the effectiveness of their new agents. In the case of the Korean War study, the Soviets concluded that the Chinese and North Korean tactic of using narcotics against the U.S. forces was extremely effective and that the USSR should adopt the Chinese tactics to "demoralize U.S. forces and to disrupt the U.S. society."

The mid- to late-1950s, however, were not a time when the Soviets were willing to start new activities that they felt the United States might be especially sensitive to, such as narcotics trafficking. At that time the Soviets were launching a major deception operation, the object of which was to end the United States' participation in the cold war and thus make Western technology and financial assistance available to the Soviet bloc. To bring about this change, the Soviet deception operation was designed to convince the West, particularly the intellectual middle class in the United States, that the Soviets had changed their ways. This was no time to initiate a new offensive operation, especially one with such negative emotional overtones as pushing illegal drugs and narcotics.

Within five years, in the summer of 1960, an appropriate opportunity to begin narcotics trafficking against the United States arose when Raúl Castro traveled to Czechoslovakia in search of aid and assistance for the new Cuba. As described by Sejna, the Soviets directed Czechoslovakia to act as an agent of the Soviet Union in covertly taking control of Fidel Castro's Cuban revolutionary government, which would be done under the cover of providing military aid and assistance. Czechoslovakia's surrogate role was operationally essential because of Fidel's distrust and dislike of the Soviets at that time and because Khrushchev was concerned that a strong Soviet presence might trigger an unfavorable U.S. reaction, which Khrushchev wanted to avoid. Thus, the Czechs were directed to begin the subversion of Cuba. Gradually, the Soviets would step in and assume control of the operation, thus establishing a new Soviet satellite before either Fidel Castro or the United States could react.

At Sejna's suggestion, an invitation was sent from Moscow to Raúl to visit the Soviet Union and meet Khrushchev. Upon his return, agreements on aid and assistance were concluded, including Cuba's consent to become a "revolutionary center" in the Western hemisphere. As part of this agreement, Czechoslovakia would "help organize" Cuban intelligence and counterintelligence. The first task assigned to Cuban intelligence, the *Dirección General de Inteligencia* (DGI), by the Soviet Union was to organize narcotics production and trafficking into the United States.

This Soviet decision in 1960 and subsequent Cuban involvement in extensive drug trafficking operations is key to understanding the narcoterrorist problem that emerged throughout Latin America in the late 1970s. Then, as now, the Soviets direct the operation for all intents and purposes. In the 1960s, while Cuba was being brought under control, Cuba did operate with a degree of "independence," even to the point of arresting some Soviet advisors and pursuing reckless revolutionary war, which was how the Soviets viewed Ernesto "Che" Guevara's activities. Accordingly, the Soviet's tightened the strings and applied extreme economic sanctions to let Castro know the extent of his dependency on the Soviets. Then, working through Raúl, those remaining anti-Soviets in Castro's entourage were purged, including DGI head Manuel Piñeiro Losada. The DGI was then placed under direct Soviet supervision. In the period since 1970, which encompasses the rise of narcoterrorism and the drive to cover the United States with "white snow," or cocaine, the DGI (the drug trafficking command center) has been totally controlled by the Soviet Union.

Information on Cuba's early narcotics trafficking was in the hands of responsible U.S. officials by 1962. The data did not generate any adverse reaction. Indeed, the dominant U.S. response to the growing drug problem—to treat the users as criminals and focus attention on the customs problem—only further alienated U.S. youth and played into Moscow's hands. The lack of U.S. response against Cuba, the growing success of the Chinese operation, and the emergence of the "drug culture" in the United States were seized upon by Moscow. The time to move into the mainstream narcotics business had arrived. In 1961 Moscow had summoned the chiefs of Eastern European intelligence services and directed them to begin collecting intelligence on drugs and drug manufacture. They were especially interested in psychochemicals, such as LSD, which formed the basis of the "tune in, turn on, and drop out" culture that was being popularized by Dr. Timothy Leary and other representatives of the U.S. drug culture.

The Warsaw Pact narcotics trafficking strategy officially began in 1962. Khrushchev summoned the top strategic leadership of the satellite countries to attend a secret meeting in Moscow in the early fall, ostensibly to discuss economic problems and budgetary cutbacks. The details on this meeting were provided by one of the official attendees. The meeting was dominated by Khrushchev, who opened the meeting with a discussion of how to combat the "negative tendencies" that were causing economic problems. Then Khrushchev turned to the drug business. Mao Tse-tung and the

Chinese were smart, he said. Though they are not as experienced as we, they are more imaginative and operative. However, Khrushchev continued, we have far better intelligence resources and should step in as fast as possible and exploit the drug business.

Khrushchev then proceeded to discuss the many advantages of the drug business. It would be a good source of much-needed foreign exchange and would finance some foreign intelligence operations. It would undermine the health and morale of U.S. soldiers and weaken the "human factor" in the defense situation. It would destroy the U.S. education system and would cause a decline in the influence of religion. In certain cases, it could be used to create chaos.

Khrushchev emphasized that the fundamental objective of the business was "to accelerate the process of demoralization of bourgeois society." The primary target was U.S. youth. The drug business was a long-term plan to undermine future bourgeois generations. The education system was a high-priority target because that was where the future bourgeois leaders were to be found. A second high-priority target was the U.S. work ethic: pride and associated loyalty. This target would also be reached through the U.S. educational system.

Khrushchev's final comment, the source recalled with great clarity, was directed at a question of morality, which evidently had been raised by some of the officials when the strategy was being formulated. To those concerns, Khrushchev stated very firmly, "But we must state categorically that anything that destroys capitalism is moral."

Following Khrushchev's instructions, individual Warsaw Pact countries set about to organize narcotics trafficking to destroy the bourgeoisie, beginning with the United States. As an example of this process, in 1962 the Czechoslovak Defense Council formally adopted and set in motion their plan to use drugs and narcotics to undermine the social fabric of the West. The plan was presented formally to the Defense Council by the minister of interior and head of the secret police, Rudolf Barak: "Not only would this action serve to destroy the Western society," he argued, "but in addition, the West will pay high prices for it." Antonín Novotný, first secretary and chairman of the Defense Council, asked how much money could be realized, and Barak responded, "Enough to finance the entire Czechoslovak intelligence service." As explained by Jan Sejna, who was the secretary of the Czechoslovak Defense Council, the narcotics and drugs business received constant attention, with progress reviews each year and improvements and coordinated plans organized by the Soviet Union almost with the same regularity.

The Chinese and Soviet narcotics war gathered significant momentum during the 1960s, which may help account for the skyrocketing growth of the U.S. narcotics problem in the 1960s. The 1960s were an era of change in the United States; many established rules were challenged. Attitudes about minorities, women's rights, sex, and social conduct were all challenged. The use of drugs also grew, partially as a result of this counterculture. More importantly, the supply (which Dr. Troiani considers the determining factor) increased and helped fuel the demand. This was also the decade that saw tremendous alienation directed at the U.S. involvement in Vietnam. From many directions, it was a decade of revolt by the youth of our country. And this discontent was seized upon and used by both the Soviets and Chinese, who waged a narcotics war against the United States—both at home and abroad (in Europe and Southeast Asia).

One of the best insights into the Chinese involvement was provided by notes that Egyptian President Gamal Abdel Nasser kept in his personal diary on meetings with the Chinese premier, Chou Enlai, in 1965. While discussing the Vietnam War and the demoralization of the U.S. forces, Chou said, "some of them are trying opium, and we are helping them. We plant the best kinds of opium especially for the American soldiers in Vietnam." Nasser's notes on the conversation were unmistakable: China was using narcotics on a large scale to demoralize U.S. troops. Chou believed the effect would be much greater than anyone could imagine. He was right.

The Chinese use of narcotics in Vietnam has been confirmed by former army intelligence operatives and Defense Department officials. China was determined to be the major source of a supply chain that snaked its way through Japan and Hong Kong into Vietnam. The operation had begun in the early 1960s, concomitant with the U.S. buildup in Vietnam. All sorts of drugs and narcotics were available, but the principal commodity in the 1960s was marijuana. Here is where the sophisticated nature of the marketing operation arises. The marijuana was not like the marijuana that had received so much publicity in the United States. This marijuana was powerful, its effects often lasting for several days. Some of the marijuana obtained this extra kick from its high residue of THC—5 percent, in contrast to the 0.5 percent typical in stateside marijuana. Additionally, much of the "harmless weed" had been dipped in opium to increase the effect and develop addicts without their knowledge.

By the end of the 1960s, drugs had become a major problem. They impaired U.S. combat effectiveness, although official estimates consistently downplayed the real nature of the problem and consequences. The United States was finally forced to take notice when, in 1970, the Chinese significantly escalated their operation. In April, President Nixon ordered the attack of sanctuaries in Cambodia. The Chinese sternly warned the United States against its "flagrant provocation." Henry Kissinger, the president's national security advisor, analyzed the Chinese response and advised the president that "the Chinese have issued a statement, in effect saying that they wouldn't do anything." Three months later, between 15 August and 15 September 1970, nearly pure heroin appeared for sale at bargain basement prices (eighty cents per gram) on the doorsteps of U.S. military installations throughout Southeast Asia. Not only that, but simultaneously the supply of marijuana and other drugs suddenly and sharply decreased.

All heroin was packaged in an identical fashion and all had come from China. Because of the low price and high quality, profit was clearly not the motive. Further, only U.S. forces were targeted. This was *political* warfare, exactly as explained to Nasser by Chou En-lai. Moreover, the timing itself, three months after the Cambodian operation, suggests that the Chinese escalation may have been in direct response to the U.S. escalation. A U.S. presidential commission was formed to investigate the matter. Their report confirmed that it was undeniably a Chinese military–intelligence operation. Rather than attract attention, the report was suppressed to avoid adversely affecting U.S. political initiatives towards China. As one of the commission members said afterwards, keeping silent about that operation was one of the "most damnable" orders he had ever received.

The efforts of the U.S. administration to play down the role of Chinese narcotics trafficking are perhaps best revealed in the distortion of the "Golden Triangle," an indiginous term for the main opium-producing region in Southeast Asia. The region encompasses mainly areas of northern Thailand, Burma, and Yunnan province in China. This region was identified by intelligence sources in 1969 when President Nixon's war on narcotics was just heating up. The map identifying the Golden Triangle evidently disturbed White House officials, because they redrew the triangle to move the corner that was high in Yunnan province down into Laos. Thus they effectively excluded the main opium-producing area in the Golden Triangle—Yunnan province in China. This political exclusion of China from the Golden Triangle is still present in the Reagan administration's description of the triangle and in its statistics on drugs and narcotics from the area.

While China was busy in Southeast Asia, the Soviet Eastern European surrogates were busy plying their trade in Europe. In 1967, with U.S. attention firmly focused on Vietnam, the Soviets decided to step up their effort. As explained by Marshal M.V. Zakharov to the Czechoslovak Defense Council, the time had come "to coordinate the production and transport and improve the operation." Accordingly, the intelligence chiefs, military and civilian, of all the Eastern European satellites were summoned to Moscow to receive their directives and develop their plans to intensify the operation.

Also in 1967, work commenced throughout the Warsaw Pact nations on the top-secret "Long-Range Plan for the Next Ten to Fifteen Years and Beyond." This plan explicitly identified the need to exploit U.S. societal vulnerabilities, in particular the growing alienation and revolt of the youth, and to intensify the use of drugs and narcotics in this effort. Intelligence organizations in all the satellite countries were explicitly charged with this task in the Soviet plan.

Jan Sejna's testimony about the Soviet-directed narcotics trafficking (undertaken as an integral part of their strategy to, as Khrushchev would say, "bury the West") remains the most comprehensive and disturbing testimony— but it does not stand alone. Much of what he has told Western intelligence agencies has been supported by other sources who also observed the process firsthand. In 1971, Stefan Sverdlev, a colonel in Bulgarian secret police (KDS) who was directly involved in their drug-running operation, defected through Greece. He brought with him some five hundred KDS documents. His knowledge, and the documents he brought with him, further confirmed the Soviet-directed operation. He also confirmed Sejna's report that the heads of Warsaw Pact secret police met in Moscow in 1967 to discuss how to "exploit and hasten the inherent 'corruption' of Western society." (In other words, how to be more effective in using narcotics in their war against the West.) He also laid out the important narcotics trafficking roles of Bulgarian intelligence and its operational front, "KINTEX," which he stated was formed in 1968. He also reported on a Bulgarian state security directive of July 1970, with the subject of "the destabilization of Western society through, among other tools, the narcotics trade."

According to former U.S. Army officials, the drug problem as it related to U.S. military personnel in Europe grew steadily more serious in the late 1960s and early 1970s. At the tail end of the distribution network, the drugs were provided by West German nationals to pushers in the U.S. Army. From the West Germans, the trail ran back through East Germany and Czechoslovakia to Bulgaria. The drugs included hashish, marijuana, heroin, and amphetamines, especially methaphetamine or "speed."

News stories of racial disturbances within the U.S. Army in Europe began to surface. In many instances, what was really taking place were drug-related territorial battles between white and black dealers. The reporting, in general, was misleading. There was also an erroneous perception within the U.S. Army chain of command: The tendency was to blame the poor quality of the recruits, rather than face up to what was happening.

One former officer explained that because President Johnson had ruled out calling up reserves for Vietnam, Europe was left with few experienced commanders and NCOs. The relative lack of experienced officers and U.S. attention on Vietnam (with its associated problems of youth and morale) created a significant vulnerability in the U.S. Army that played into the hands of the Soviet narcotics strategy.

By 1973 the problem had become so severe that a serious breakdown in the U.S. Army chain of command was feared. It was then that the top echelons in the U.S. Army in Europe began to treat the problem as something more than a social problem. Together with the West German authorities, they began to take action. Various disciplinary actions were taken, including the transfers of numerous soldiers, some of whom were returned to the states and were discharged. A major battle was waged against trafficking networks in 1973 and 1974. But though these actions may have restored the command integrity, they did not address the real problem. As soon as one distribution chain was broken, another quickly emerged to maintain the traffic.

One of the best examples of why the problem exists and has continued to grow (despite concern from the highest levels of the U.S. government and major efforts to deal with it) is the approach taken by the U.S. Customs Service to suppress the European drug trafficking. Since 1970 there has been a stream of consistent data on Bulgaria's drug trafficking activities and the role of KINTEX, a "commercial" trading firm that is a Bulgarian intelligence front for narcotics trafficking, gunrunning, and other nefarious activities. Notwithstanding this knowledge, in November 1971 the U.S. customs and the Bureau of Narcotics and Dangerous Drugs concluded a tentative agreement with Bulgarian customs. The U.S. authorities initiated this action in order to exchange information and to provide U.S. training for Bulgarian customs officials to improve Bulgaria's ability to interdict illicit drugs crossing its borders. U.S. customs actually initiated a series of training seminars at the Bulgarian customs training school in 1973, with repeat sessions in 1974 and 1975. They also provided intelligence on suspected and known traffickers and their techniques to the Bulgarians.

It was not until the fall of 1981 that the U.S. officials determined that they really were not receiving Bulgaria's complete support and decided to suspend the operation. But even there the saga does not end. As recently as 1984, these same U.S. officials stated that they "continue to have hopes of convincing the Bulgarian Government to bring a halt to arms and narcotics trafficking."

Scenario Eleven: Managua, Nicaragua

"Manolo, my friend," the Nicaraguan Comandante said, rising from his desk to greet the visitor. He crossed the large richly decorated office and gave the visitor—a Latin dressed in dark slacks and a guayabera—a warm abrazo. The walls of the office were lined with crucifixes of every description. Although the Comandante was a nonbeliever, he had started collecting crucifixes some years earlier, intrigued by their value as antiques and precious relics. Since taking power, his collection had grown by leaps and bounds, as no visitor in need of a favor could neglect to bring along a crucifix as a gift for the Comandante. It was said that every museum-quality crucifix that had come on the market anywhere in Latin America during the previous five years had ended up in the Comandante's collection.

"You wanted to see me, Señor Comandante?" Manolo asked as the Comandante showed him to a seat in front of his massive desk. A jagged scar, which he had received in a Mexican prison fight, ran from the corner of Manolo's mouth to his ear.

The Comandante was wearing a freshly starched and pressed uniform with no adornment, and a Soviet-made Makarov pistol on his hip. His dark skin was shiny. It was stretched so tightly across his skull that it gave him a reptilian look. He was small, almost tiny, and he seemed to disappear in the oversized, high-backed chair behind the desk. But if he looked like a child behind a grownup's desk, his voice was a large man's voice, full of authority, the type of voice that sways and moves other men.

"Thank you for coming on such short notice," he began. "However, I'm afraid I've got some bad news."

"What is it, Comandante?" asked Manolo apprehensively, leaning forward to hear better.

"You and your colleagues have enjoyed the protection of this government for some time. We permit you to operate with little or no interference. You process your drugs here, and use our harbors and airstrips for your boats and planes. We even provide you with intelligence data and, when needed, diplomatic cover. You make millions of dollars running drugs into the United States." He turned and spat into the wastebasket as if he had to get a bad taste out of

his mouth. Then he resumed, "And what do we get for our generosity?"

Manolo did not answer. He couldn't figure out what the Comandante was driving at.

"I'll tell you what we get," announced the Comandante. "In addition to the fees you pay us, and shipments of arms you carry to our friends helping us in the struggle against U.S. imperialism, every pound of cocaine or bale of marijuana you smuggle into the United States"—he spat again into the wastebasket—"weakens old 'Uncle Alligator,' speeds his decadent disintegration, and corrupts his youth and military." He smiled and picked at his teeth with his forefinger. "We cannot fight the United States directly, but we can speed its destruction from within."

"That's right, Comandante," Manolo agreed. "It is a privilege to be at your side in the fight against imperialism." As Manolo had estates in six countries, a private jet, a yacht, a fleet of exotic cars, and a $25,000 round bed and video entertainment center where he frolicked with his mistresses, he decided to leave out the line about how proud he was to contribute to the spread of Marxism-Leninism and the ultimate victory of the proletariat. Quite frankly, he just didn't feel like a member of the proletariat anymore.

"But this symbiotic relationship we have established is today jeopardized," the Comandante continued. "Until recently everything seemed to be going our way. Many members of the U.S. Congress wanted to believe we are mere social reformers"—he spat once again into the wastebasket—" so we methodically cultivated that impression while we consolidated our power. And we found the Yanqui press willing to help us." He held up a framed picture of a neurotic woman reporter from a leading U.S. daily. He humorously recalled her captivation over the experience of sleeping with a real revolutionary like the Comandante, and how she accordingly had filed misleading and distorted stories about the Sandinistas for more than two years.

"All we have accomplished is now threatened by disclosures to Congress about our assistance to you and your friends." The Comandante shook his head sadly. "There is a member of the U.S. National Security Council staff who won't give up. He keeps digging up new information, much of which is very embarrassing to us and

damaging to our international image. If he can conclusively link us to drug trafficking, he may just be able to win enough support in the U.S. Congress to overcome the objections of our friends regarding aid for the Contras."

"Who is this man, Comandante?"

The Comandante pushed a manila folder across his desk. Manolo picked up the folder. He studied a photograph of a man in a military uniform and then began to read the data.

"If the drug thing blows up in our faces," the Comandante said, peering through slit-like eyes at the drug lord, his words carefully chosen, his manner deliberate and calculated, "then, my friend, you're out of business. We won't be able to provide you with safe haven and logistics support any more."

"That would be terrible, Comandante," Manolo exclaimed, genuinely alarmed. Then added: "For all of us."

The Comandante acknowledged Manolo's words with a slight nod of his head.

"You say that it is all because of this one man?" Manolo resumed, holding up the photograph from the file.

"Not entirely, of course. But he's the biggest part of the problem. It is said he has great conviction and energy, and I understand he is a favorite of the American President." The Comandante knew he had Manolo hooked; now it was time to reel him in. "If only he would retire, or . . ."

"Could we make him a business offer?" Manolo interrupted.

"Money?" The Comandante laughed. "No, he's much too straight and upright for that."

"Perhaps he could meet with an accident?"

The Comandante did not respond immediately. He let the words take on added import by his silence.

Manolo got the message. "It will be done, Comandante," he announced. He rose and gave the Comandante a toothy grin, then left without further ado.

The Comandante noticed that Manolo had left something on the corner of the desk, wrapped in tissue paper. It was a gold chain with a jewel-encrusted crucifix dangling from it. He smiled as he fingered the newest addition to his collection. He reflected on the fate of the NSC pig who was about to learn what revolutionary war

*was all about. It was all so easy. If Manolo botched the job, the
Comandante would deny, on behalf of his government, any involvement in the affair and accuse the CIA of engineering the whole thing
to discredit the Nicaraguan government. There would be plenty of
fools in the American Congress and media, useful idiots Lenin had
called them, who would be willing to believe his accusations over
the denials of the CIA. Besides, denials could never be verified.*

In that case, he would simply find another assassin.

Narcoterrorism

The integration of narcotics trafficking and terrorism since the mid-
1970s or early 1980s has strengthened the hand of both the terrorists and the narcotics traffickers. This union provides terrorists with
an ample supply of money, guns, and explosives; it provides the
narcotics traffickers with security, sanctuary, and protection. And it
has introduced a major new destabilizing force in countries of all
levels of development, undermining law and order, subverting leadership, and creating revolutionary situations for Marxist-Leninist
takeovers.

The marriage of terrorism and narcotics is only natural: Both
are unprincipled and lawless; they are complementary rather than
competitive; both are in large measure the product of communist
strategic intelligence operations; and as such they have a common
objective—to bring down the established order. For a period of
time, from the early 1960s to the mid-1970s, the two appeared to
travel separate, albeit parallel paths. In the late 1970s, the two
merged, the union blossomed, and the practice rapidly spread to all
areas of the globe.

The practice received its first major publicity on 5 November
1982, when four aides to Fidel Castro were indicted by a federal
grand jury on charges of conspiring to bring narcotics into the
United States illegally. These included a senior official in the DGI
who was a ranking member of the Central Committee of the Communist Party of Cuba and president of the Cuban Institute of
Friendship, also known as the ICAP; a vice admiral in the Cuban

Navy and member of the Central Committee; the Cuban ambassador to Colombia; and a former minister-counselor of the Cuban Embassy in Colombia. The witnesses testifying for the U.S. government at the trial in Miami federal court had been firsthand participants. They included a DGI agent smuggled into the United States; a drug smuggler who brought the drugs from Cuba into the United States; and a lawyer-turned-smuggler who helped arrange the transactions between Colombia, where the drugs were produced, and Cuba.

Beginning in 1979, Jaime Guillot-Lara (one of the major drug dealers operating out of Colombia, whose activities were the subject of the indictment) negotiated a deal with Cuba whereby Guillot-Lara's ships transporting drugs and narcotics were guaranteed protection and safe haven in Cuban waters and facilities for repair, rest, storage, and transfer of the goods to fast boats for delivery to the United States. In return, Guillot-Lara paid Cuba a fee of $800,000 per delivery and on his return trip would transport guns and explosives to terrorist and revolutionary war forces in Latin America, particularly Nicaragua and Colombia. In one instance, the Colombian Navy sank a Guillot-Lara ship, the *Karina,* loaded with one hundred tons of weapons. In another incident, the *Monarca* was seized just after it landed a large shipment of weapons destined for the M-19 revolutionary terrorists.

Columbia, the South American capital of drug trafficking, is a good example of how the system operates. Within Colombia, there are three main revolutionary organizations: the Revolutionary Armed Forces of Colombia, or FARC; the Nineteenth of April Movement, known as the M-19 revolutionaries; and the Latin National Movement. The M-19 revolutionaries are the strongest and best equipped. They are directly aligned with and supported by the Soviet Union, operating through Cuba. Guillot-Lara had close ties to the M-19, whose leader, Jaime Bateman, is reported to have promised Guillot-Lara a position when a Marxist government is formed in Colombia. Guillot-Lara also was identified as assisting with a Cuba–M-19 plot to invade Colombia. Guillot-Lara provided transportation for guns and M-19 forces to southern Colombia.

The revolutionaries protect the drug production sanctuaries. They attack government forces that come too close, and they warn the producers of raids and related police action. In the early 1980s, in response to U.S. pressure, Colombian officials have sought to oppose the drug traffickers. The revolutionaries countered by murdering and assassinating key government officials and their staffs. In 1984 Justice Minister Rodrigo Lara Bonilla and former Assistant Minister Eduardo Gonzalez were gunned down. Lara was a highly visible leader of the government's antinarcotics campaign, and Gonzalez was supporting U.S. extradition actions against Colombian drug dealers.

Carlos Lehder Rivas, one of the larger Colombian drug exporters, spoke out on the cooperation between the drug industry and the Latin American revolutionaries. The assassination of Justice Minister Lara was justified, he said. When asked if he would support a military government, Lehder said he would, but "only if the army were a *popular* army. . . ." When asked about the use of an island he owns in the Bahamas for refueling planes carrying cocaine to the United States, he denied any involvement in the drug business. (There is a warrant for his arrest and the United States has requested extradition.) He then went on to say, "The question today no longer is whether there is drug dealing or not, whether this produces a bonanza or not, or who profits from the bonanza. This bonanza is a *revolutionary means of struggle against imperialism* and against the monarchical oligarchy. . . . Cocaine is the Latin American Atom Bomb"[emphasis added].

Mario Estevez Gonzalez was a DGI agent who defected and gave important evidence at the Miami trial. Estevez was one of three thousand DGI agents infiltrated into Florida during the Mariel boatlift of 1980. The boatlift, he testified, had been in the planning for several years. It was not a makeshift operation as it so often has been described in the U.S. news media. His mission was to penetrate and sabotage the anti-Castro organization in Florida known as Alpha 66. After destroying considerable equipment and sinking two Alpha 66 boats, he was assigned a new mission by his DGI superior: drug trafficking. He was told that it was "important to load up the United States with drugs."

Estevez explained that Cuba had been in the drug trafficking business—growing, producing, buying, shipping, and selling—for many years, "back to Vietnam days," he said, adding that this was a very secret operation. No one except the DGI and Fidel Castro knew of the operation. The Cuban people were ignorant of the operation; they are strongly opposed to the use of drugs, which is a major crime in Cuba. Cuba also received cocaine, which was funneled to the United States, as payment by guerrillas sent to Cuba for training in the Cuban terrorist and guerrilla training camps that had been established in the late 1960s. Estevez and other DGI defectors also clearly identified the Soviet presence and their direct management and funding of the DGI since 1970.

Defectors from the Sandinista regime in Nicaragua have testified about the strong presence of Cuban, Soviet, and Eastern European advisors throughout their government. These advisors, especially the Soviets and Cubans, are said to dominate the decision-making process. In 1982–83, Nicaragua set itself up in the narcotics trafficking business. The Nicaraguan involvement has been confirmed by former high-ranking Nicaraguan officials. One, Antonio Farach, described the operation as political warfare directed against U.S. youth.

The Nicaraguan plot was hatched in a meeting between Raúl Castro and Umberto Ortega, the Nicaraguan defense minister and brother of Daniel Ortega. The operation was built up under the direction of Tomás Borge, interior minister and head of Nicaraguan intelligence. By 1984, Nicaragua had reached an agreement with two major Colombian traffickers to use Nicaragua in their cocaine smuggling operation. Manufacturing supplies were flown in from the United States and the chemicals were shipped from Europe via Havana.

In the summer of 1983 U.S. customs was alerted that the vessel *Charisma* would carry the product to the United States. The ship was located and seized two months later. In its hold were computers and communications equipment being smuggled to Cuba. The captain, James Herring, told a story of both high-tech smuggling and drug smuggling that the U.S. officials were disinclined to believe because it all sounded so "outrageous." Herring implicated a Netherlands smuggler, Ube Dekker, in a web of activities involving cocaine; Nicaragua; Borge; the U.S. fugitive Robert Vesco; what would appear to be a Nicaraguan counterpart to Bulgaria's KINTEX that was called SEBIMEX; distribution chains from Europe to

Nicaragua to America; landing strips in the Bahamas; and so forth. Herring testified freely. His knowledge was especially pertinent because he had been hired by Nicaragua to help them set up their cocaine operation, especially the selection of planes, landing strips, and the cocaine-cutting lab itself. Dekker also testified and confirmed the operation, participants, and involvement of the Nicaraguan intelligence and party officials, and their plans to grow marijuana, which was to be converted to hashish. In response to a question of whether the operation was merely the activity of a few corrupt officials, he responded, "Completely doubtful, it's impossible."

Robert Vesco has also been linked to Pablo Escobar Gaviria, a former deputy in the Colombian House of Representatives. Escobar now is on the "wanted" list of several countries, including his own. He operates out of Cuba, where his secure base is believed to be on the islet of Piedra, off the northern coast of Cuba. Escobar travels frequently to Nicaragua—always in Cuban Air Force planes. Vesco is reportedly his chief of staff. In addition to helping Cuba in the organization and recruiting of drug traffickers, Escobar and Vesco have helped the Cubans acquire high-velocity diesel-powered launches and have organized an information network for Castro's arms traffic.

The South American countries that have been most heavily involved in narcotics and drug trafficking, in addition to Colombia, are Bolivia and Peru, where coca leaves are harvested and processed (or exported for processing abroad) into cocaine. Here, the impact of the narcoterrorism merger is especially noticeable, The cocaine dealers, through their money and the muscle provided by their terrorist sidekicks, have become dominant figures. They are able to buy or intimidate government officials and generally operate outside the law. The intimidation is brutal. In Colombia, eighteen months after Justice Minister Lara and Assistant Minister Gonzalez were gunned down, all twelve Supreme Court justices were executed (one bullet into the head of each justice) during a bloody siege of the Palace of Justice. Bogotá's leading newspaper reported that Carlos Lehder Rivas paid the M-19 revolutionaries $4 million for that service.

The list of other examples is impressive: Officials of all ranks, from policemen to the president, have been kidnapped, maimed, and murdered. Terrorists and drug dealers have started their own newspapers and formed independent political parties. In Peru, the Maoist Sendero Luminoso (Shining Path) guerrillas have organized the coca growers and provide protection. The situation in Bolivia— one of rampant drug-money corruption—is reflected in the highly publicized U.S.–Bolivian raid on 24 July 1986, which featured the capture of a giant cocaine lab. According to intelligence sources, what the newspapers failed to grasp was that this was a "media event." There were no arrests, no casualties, no cocaine or coca— only residue. The raid was conducted during the traditional pro-duction vacation time. The equipment seized was old and obsolete. The jungle narcotics lab was really a sacrificial offering to show cooperation and progress in combating the drug problem. More im-pressive and realistic is the testimony before Senator Paula Haw-kin's Drug and Alcohol Abuse subcommittee in 1985: Bolivia is cor-rupted with drug money. Cultivation and production have been expanding. "Bolivia seems to be developing a large-scale hydrochlo-ride [cocaine] processing capability both to supply the United States consumers and, in concert with Argentina, Brazilian, and Chilean groups, to develop and service a rapidly growing European market."

Closer to home, Mexico has become perhaps *the* major conduit of drugs into the United States. In a country where the political leaders are but barely able to maintain a semblance of control, this does not bode well, either for the United States or for Mexico. The drug influence can be seen in Mexico's handling of Guillot-Lara. He had been arrested and held in a Mexican jail. He was released, the Mexican government refused to extradite him, and he disappeared.

Since 1985, drug dealers have deliberately tortured, then mur-dered, U.S. Drug Enforcement Agency (DEA) officers who are op-erating against the drug networks in Mexico with the permission of the Mexican government. The corruption that accompanies the drug business was illustrated in the 1986 case of DEA agent Victor Cortez, Jr. Cortez was kidnapped by Jalisco State Police and taken to a Jalisco State Police detention center where he was stripped, beaten, and tortured with electric cattle prods. The Mexican police wanted to extract the identities of other DEA agents working in Mexico from Cortez. There is little doubt that Cortez would have ended up dead (as his colleague, Enrique Comarena Salazar, who was tortured, then murdered, in February 1985) had his kidnapping not been witnessed by two other DEA agents. They traced the license numbers of the unmarked cars and reported the event to their boss, Tony Ayala. Ayala surrounded the detention center for more than six hours until Cortez's release could be secured—reportedly only on the order of President de la Madrid.

The marriage of narcoterrorist and narcorevolutionary forces is not limited to Latin America. On the other side of the globe, in Burma and Malaysia, communist terrorists have incorporated the use of narcotics both to fund their activities and to destabilize the countries they seek to take over. In the Golden Triangle of Southeast Asia, the Burmese Communist Party and Shan United Army terrorists have joined ranks in their bid for Burma. In Thailand, the Communist Party of Thailand engages in drug-related activities. Printed instructions from the Socialist Republic of Vietnam to farmers on where to obtain poppy seeds and when to plant them were passed to the West. In the Middle East, the Marxist group known as the Justice Commandos of the Armenian Genocide has teamed with the Armenian hashish dealer Noubar Sofoyan (who has close ties to Lebanon) for attacks on Turkey. Slightly to the south, the Syrians are not defending the Bekaa Valley just to protect their flank from the Israelis. Rather, they are protecting their multibillion dollar hashish and heroin smuggling routes. In Europe, the Red Brigades have been tied to the narcotics problem in Italy; in Ireland and northern Great Britain, drug addiction suddenly shot up during the early 1980s.

Drugs are being used around the world to destabilize societies, finance terrorist operations, and corrupt local officials—which in turn encourages further destabilization and terrorist operations. Narcoterrorism creates power while it feeds on and destroys the power of the established political order. As their power base grows, and that of the host nation shrinks, the narcoterrorists act with greater impunity. In effect, the narcoterrorists are given a free ride. And whenever they choose to bring about a revolution, the base will be ready. In the meantime, there is no real hurry, and the existing governments provide an ideal combination of cover and scapegoat. The narcoterrorists can continue their operations at will. For all practical purposes, the revolution has already begun; the people merely do not recognize the process. This is why the rise of Mexico as the major conduit for drugs into the United States is so portentous.

Nor is the trafficking limited to natural products such as marijuana, cocaine, and heroin. The trafficking also includes bulk synthetics such as methaqualone, used in the manufacture of pills commonly known by their trade name, Quaalude. Methaqualone is shipped in from pharmaceutical plants in Eastern Europe and the People's Republic of China to production sites in Colombia. There it is made into pills and packaged for distribution to the United States. The drugs are smuggled into the United States either directly from the production areas with transshipment points in Nicaragua and Cuba, or indirectly through Canada, Mexico, and the Bahamas, with the tacit complicity of certain officials in these countries.

Though the enormity of this problem has begun to surface since the early 1980s, many important gaps remain. Most importantly, attention has yet to focus on the brain behind the major portion of the narcoterrorist operations—the Soviet Union. In addition to the direct and obvious activities of Cuba's DGI, which is run by the Soviet Union, there is an even more important covert role. Beginning in 1962, Cuban intelligence, with the assistance of Soviet bloc intelligence services where appropriate, was directed to infiltrate and control all Latin American drug operations, from production to distribution. In the process, they were to collect data on the drug-associated corruption to use in blackmail and intimidation. By 1968, nearly all of the Latin American drug operations had been penetrated. Planning within the communist intelligence circles had become focused on destroying the remaining drug operators who would not join with the Soviet-directed operation. Most recently, a good example is provided by the rapidity with which Nicaragua, the most recent Marxist-Leninist recruit, entered the drug trafficking business in the early 1980s. In this connection, Afghanistan, traditionally a supplier, was working to eradicate its trafficking before the Soviets invaded in December 1979. However, Afghanistan has dramatically increased its production and trafficking since 1981. It is a serious error not to recognize the behind-the-scenes organization directed by the Soviet Administrative Organs Department and the strategic intelligence sections of the KGB and GRU.

A second apparent gap is the absence of almost any mention of the People's Republic of China in the current reports on narcotics trafficking. In a rare instance, China was identified, along with Eastern Europe, as a major supplier of methaqualone. But though China's Yunnan province has traditionally been the major heroin producer in the Golden Triangle, State Department and DEA reports on poppy cultivation and heroin and opium production do not even list China as part of the Golden Triangle.

China's role, traditionally, has been quite different from most other operations because production in China has been carried on in numerous large and small pharmaceutical plants, which may help explain their role in the methaqualone trafficking. In the early 1970s, reports from the Far East detailed millions of acres under cultivation; forty-seven large and twenty-five small processing plants; nineteen brands of opium, twelve of morphine, and thirteen of heroin; seven major trade routes; and a gross income from trafficking into Southeast Asia of over $1 billion between 1966 and 1971. It seems somewhat naive, or overly optimistic, to assume that this has all gone away.

Narcotics Warfare and National Security

The impact of drug use on national security is easy to appreciate. The drug habit, once developed, is expensive. Within the national security industry, the habit provides a potential espionage vulnerability as addicts turn to the sales of military secrets to support the financial needs that are part of the addicts' baggage. Drug use also impairs the senses, by design. This disruptive effect can last for days and impair an individual's ability to maintain concentration or perform difficult tasks. Even extremely low dose levels can have major effects when coupled with mental or physical stress. And, as experienced most vividly during the 1960s, drug abuse leads to a sense of alienation within society, especially among the youth and underprivileged, who constitute a significant portion of the military forces.

If the above were not bad enough, there is still another dimension that has yet to be discussed. This is the use of narcotics and drugs as a mechanism for distributing biochem agents to specific users or user groups. As easily as marijuana can be contaminated by adding opium, so can C/B agents be added to drugs or narcotics by people handling the supply or distribution of the drugs. Such a deliberate addition could be designed to produce profound effects on the user without the user's knowledge or even suspicion. Needless to say, users of illegal drugs rarely complain about the quality of the product to law-enforcement officers or to their bosses.

The possibility of lacing drugs with sinister biochem creations is frightening. Consider, for example the spread of disease. Bacteria or viruses (for example the AIDS virus) could be freeze-dried and incorporated into drug capsules or heroin packets. Similarly, miscreants could introduce toxins or special high-potency drugs that have long-lasting negative effects on mental or physical processes. Such additives would be extremely difficult to detect unless the medical doctor or epidemiologist knew in advance precisely what to look for.

The potential for mischief is enormous when the number of drug and narcotics users is considered. Today, there are estimated to be more than twenty million Americans who use marijuana regularly; between eight and twenty million who use cocaine regularly; one-half million who are active heroin addicts; one million who use hallucinogenics; and about six million who use fraudulently obtained prescription drugs. Two trends in these statistics are especially grim: "the spread of cocaine to all levels of the social spectrum and the growing number of young users," as Attorney General Edwin Meese testified before Congress in 1985.

Surveys of drug usage among U.S. servicemen stationed abroad during the early 1980s confirm a pervasive level of chemical dependency, generally consistent with the frequency of drug use within the United States. The official 1982 Pentagon health services study reported that 31.4 percent of U.S. servicemen in Europe who were polled admitted using drugs (including marijuana, cocaine, and LSD) the preceding year. Depending on the service and the location, 15–47 percent of the sampled servicemen were drug users. Those statistics triggered a major effort to bring drug use in the military under control, and at the last poll, the figures had dropped to the vicinity of 10 percent. Nevertheless, the situation remains critical. In 1984, a drug raid at Fort Belvoir, south of Washington, D.C., netted seventy servicemen who were charged with crimes ranging from possession of cocaine to selling marijuana. In 1984, 35,514 army soldiers tested positively for drug use, as did 8,055 members of the air force, and 60,024 navy personnel. Moreover, even these statistics can be misleading. The tests do not identify users of the new "designer drugs" that have been on the increase in California since 1979, nor do the tests indicate what might happen during a crisis situation.

The potential for sabotage is immense. For example, on 23 November 1969, four Strategic Air Command (SAC) officers and a mechanic at Castle Air Force Base, California, were arrested for drug trafficking. They "were responsible for surveillance of western airspace and were on continuous alert to fly missions with nuclear weapons." Investigators found 17.2 grams of marijuana and assorted drugs in the quarters of one officer. A picture of Ho Chi Minh hung on the wall of his room.

Over the summer of 1969, the army had become concerned about the use of drugs at various installations, particularly the nuclear Nike–Hercules air defense sites. On 3 October, ten officers and soldiers were arrested at the air defense site at Homestead Air Force Base in Florida. On October 5, a Cuban MG-15 made a surprise landing at Homestead and, much to everyone's chagrin, taxied right up to Air Force One, which was waiting to take President Nixon back from Key Biscayne. Both personnel and crew of the Nike–Hercules batteries stationed there—twenty-five people in all—were high. All were arrested for marijuana and LSD use.

In 1970, a counterintelligence agent conducting an investigation at Fort Dix, New Jersey, found that 75 percent of the GIs smoked marijuana; 55 percent took LSD or Methedrine once a week; and 30–35 percent took them several times a week. In the mid-1970s, army intelligence broke a hashish network that was using the U.S. Army postal service in West Germany as their distribution network.

Skipping ahead to the present, the event that caught the attention of all the uniformed services was the crash of a navy jet fighter while attempting to land on the USS *Nimitz* in 1981. Fourteen servicemen were killed. Autopsies performed on the pilot and deck crew revealed evidence of illicit drug use in both the pilot and members of the crew.

A good example of the manner in which chemicals can be used, and of the difficulty in understanding what is happening, occurred at an isolated location in West Germany, in the winter of 1975. Over a hundred military personnel were brought together to form a sensitive command and control unit in a mock war plans exercise.

The work site, a collection of tents and equipment vans, was manned around the clock by two twelve-hour shifts, each composed of about forty personnel. Shortly after the 7:00 A.M. shift began, several soldiers reported uncomfortable feelings and light-headedness. The onset seemed to correspond with the testing of the power system; it was thought that the work area had been contaminated with toxic fumes. The work site was evacuated, but the officers judged the air to be safe; accordingly, the site was reoccupied and the military exercise was continued.

Within two hours, several members of the shift had to be sent to the local dispensary. Ultimately, eighteen soldiers, nearly half of the duty staff, were incapacitated. The U.S. Army General Hospital at Landstuhl was notified of the large number of individuals suffering from an unknown illness. Five physicians were placed on a helicopter and rushed to the dispensary. Numerous tests were run and detailed interviews conducted to determine what had happened. Nearly all the victims had experienced light-headedness; decreased ability to concentrate; difficulty in thinking; feelings of unreality; changes in mood; unstable behavior; feeling of separation of mind and body; double vision; and other symptoms. All indicators pointed to the morning breakfast or coffee, but there were no leftovers to be tested.

The routine lab tests were generally unrewarding. It was not until fifteen days after the incident, when the results of specialized urine tests were completed, that firm evidence of what might have happened was available. Tests showed that sixteen of the eighteen urine samples tested positively for LSD, leading to the conclusion of mass LSD intoxication.

How it happened still is unknown, although the prime suspect is the coffee urn. Although the situation was likely the result of an unwise prank, it illustrates an important vulnerability—one that has caused problems even to the extremely security-conscious Israeli military forces. In 1984 the coffee at an Israeli officers' mess was contaminated with carbamate, one of the first nerve agents.

None of the examples cited involve the use of new, sophisticated drugs and agents made possible by the recent advances in biochemistry, neuropharmacology, and molecular biology. When such advances are considered, the possibilities become far more sophisticated, deadly, and perhaps even impossible to diagnose—particularly in time to do some good.

One of the newer complications confronting both civil and military authorities is the spread of "designer drugs," high-tech heroin substitutes. These drugs are synthetics designed to mimic heroin—hence the name designer drugs. The drugs are exceedingly potent. The newest ones are up to four thousand times more potent than heroin, and because they are new, they are not illegal. When one drug is identified and declared illegal, less than a month goes by before a new modified—and legal—variant or analogue surfaces to take its place. And the process continues. The first fentanyl analogue, alpha-methyl-fentanyl, appeared in 1979 in Orange County, California. Since 1981, DEA laboratories have identified seven more fentanyl analogues. Authorities in California now estimate that 20 percent of heroin addicts are using the fentanyl analogues.

One of the authorities in the field, Dr. Gary Henderson (a pharmacologist and toxicologist at the University of California, Davis), believes that a world-class medicinal chemist has been responsible for the many analogues of fentanyl that have appeared. The analogues have been very carefully selected to meet the drug users' needs. They are very well prepared, and appear to use a highly efficient reaction scheme not in the published literature. The drugs are very pure, and the doses are very uniform. The thinking, Henderson concludes, is of an order of magnitude above that of the classic amphetamine or PCP chemist. The quality is comparable to what one might expect if the source were a pharamaceutical plant rather than a clandestine basement laboratory. The unaddressed question is this: Could not the drugs have come from a pharma-ceutical plant, such as those supplying methaqualone to the drug trafficking chain that originates in Colombia? Or, alternatively, might they not be suppliers in the future?

Because the designer drugs are so potent, tracking the sub-stances down is exceedingly difficult and getting worse. A two-hundred gram batch of fentanyl (less than half a pound) represents a lifetime supply of two hundred *million* doses. This potency also greatly magnifies the difficulty of detecting evidence of use in the bloodstream or urine. Extremely sensitive laboratory techniques are required to detect such drugs—techniques capable of detecting con-centrations of a few parts per billion. The drugs are astronomically more profitable than heroin. This explains why the supply of these designer drugs can be expected to expand. An investment of $2,000 translates into a street value of over $1 billion.

Along even more sophisticated lines, harmless biological organ-isms could be modified by adding special genes to their DNA, genes that are responsible for the production of chemicals that influence the mind or regulate biological processes. These are areas where the Soviets have focused major research efforts. Applying the results of this research to drug distribution networks (which have come in-creasingly under the control of Soviet surrogate or pro-Soviet or-ganizations), or even to common food and drink supplies, opens new vistas for sabotage that have been considered by few, if any, of those officials who are charged with protecting the nation and its military forces against sabotage.

5
CBW Proliferation: An Even More Dangerous World

CBW Comes of Age

The number of countries with offensive C/B warfare (CBW) capabilities is at a historic high. The State Department estimates that there are ten to twelve such countries. The Chemical Warfare Review Commission appointed by the president estimated there were sixteen such countries in 1985. Private experts suggest the number is closer to twenty-five. Before the end of the century, the number easily could be fifty.

What is causing this growth? The main reason is simple: self-preservation. Nations are not always blind to a threat, and today many realize that the threat of CBW is here to stay. Accordingly, the only prudent course of action is to become prepared.

The threat has been growing since 1963, when reports first surfaced in the Middle East about the use of chemical agents by Egyptian forces fighting as Soviet proxies against rebels in Yemen. This is the same time that the Soviet Union decided that C/B weapons would be extremely important in the future and began a major push to expand their CBW capability. This was also when the Soviets decided they would use C/B weapons in the Third World.

The Middle East was the first area to feel the sting of the new Soviet policy. First, there was Yemen, where the use of chemical weapons was reported during the period 1963–67. Second, the specter of chemical warfare was brought home to Israel when nerve agent shells were discovered among the munitions captured in the Sinai desert during the Six-Day War. Third, Iraq's interest emerged in 1967. As reported by the former secretary of the Czechoslovak Defense Council, Jan Sejna, Iraq learned that Israel was acquiring nuclear weapons and asked the Soviet Union for nuclear weapons to counteract the Israeli threat. The Soviets balked at this suggestion, and, instead, decided to provide Iraq with C/B agents. This decision was made in the fall of 1967. At that time, the only question was what intermediary to use in passing the agents to Iraq so as to hide the Soviet source.

After a brief respite, concern again focused on the Middle East in June 1973 during the Yom Kippur War. Egypt was reportedly prepared to employ C/B munitions, which were associated with SCUD deployments and bombs poised for use against Israel. This concern grew especially serious when analyses of captured Soviet equipment revealed that it had been designed for fighting in contaminated environments. Collective protection, filters, garments, and medical treatment kits—all were present and upon analysis were determined to be superior to U.S equipment, which had been neglected and allowed to deteriorate.

The Soviet equipment that had been provided to the Egyptians (and the rumors of various offensive munitions) might have been ignored had it not been for the massive use, beginning in 1975 and continuing until 1984, of a wide variety of old and new chemical agents in Southeast Asia and Afghanistan, and again in the Middle East beginning in 1983. The decade 1975–85 was indeed the break-out decade. Nine nations would ultimately be directly involved: the Soviet Union, Laos, Kampuchea, Vietnam, Thailand, China, Afghanistan, Iran, and Iraq.

The first reports on what was to become known as Yellow Rain emanated from Laos in 1975. As subsequently described by a Lao People's Liberation Army officer defector, these were code-named "extinct destruction operations." The operations were undertaken with the assistance of Vietnamese officers and carried out under extreme secrecy against the Hmong. Reports and data on these activities were initially disregarded by U.S. personnel stationed in the area. The symptomatology did not match that of known CBW agents; there was no interest in the data; and there was no intelligence requirement to collect the data. Dr. Amos Townsend, a physician working in refugee camps, compared the situation to that of 1945, when no one wanted to believe the stories about concentration camps in Germany. But the reports continued, and in 1979, similar stories began filtering out of Kampuchea immediately following Vietnam's invasion of that country.

Following the Soviet Union's massive occupation of Afghanistan in December 1979 similar reports came from that country and its refugees: more Yellow Rain, more victims, and, especially ominous, reports on what appeared to be the experimental use of devastating new chemical agents. In addition to reports, there was direct testimony from both Afghan and Soviet defectors. An Afghan pilot described the use of chemicals that made the skin so soft that a person's finger could punch right through it. A Soviet soldier testified that he knew of three chemical agents that were stored there: picric acid, various asphyxiating gases, and a chemical described as "100 percent lethal.'

By the end of 1982, the State Department had documented 278 CBW attacks in Laos; 141 attacks in Kampuchea and along the Thai–Kampuchea border; and 59 attacks in Afghanistan. The combined death toll was over ten thousand. These were the totals for data that was obtained *after* people began collecting and analyzing reports on the attacks—data obtained before the intelligence priority for the collection of such data was elevated to a meaningful level.

The collection of adequate data was made even more difficult because the U.S. government did not know until 1980 what agents were involved. The agents were finally identified only because an army civilian researcher, Dr. Sharon Watson, had an appropriate background in the little-known field of mycotoxins, and decided to test for their presence. This process has been further complicated by careless data collection procedures and by faulty analytical techniques employed by the army's Chemical Research Development Center.

All in all, the collection, analysis, and presentation of results was, at best, a confused mess. This is one reason why numerous academics and members of the arms control community have challenged the data and looked for other possible explanations, the bee-dung theory advanced by Harvard's Matthew Meselson being the most notable. A more fundamental reason, however, is that many arms control proponents knew full well the implications flowing from verified Soviet use of chemical and mycotoxin weapons. Not only would this shatter the C/B arms control treaties in which they had invested so much effort, but such verification would likely stimulate new research and development of similar weapons by the United States. Still others feared that their professions—biochemistry and genetic engineering— might suffer the stigma that had been attached to nuclear physics and nuclear physicists following the development of the atomic and hydrogen bombs.

The tireless efforts of the academic and arms control enthusiasts nearly succeeded. The Soviets, moreover, appeared to put the brakes on their chemical warfare activity before the United States could initiate an aggressive effort to collect more dramatic "smoking gun" evidence. The clincher was that enough other nations had gotten into the act and were independently, if informally, confirming the U.S. government findings. More importantly, nations in proximity to the danger were not sidetracked by academic demands for legal evidence and laboratory procedures. They could count the casualties and the dead. They knew firsthand the nature of the enemy and Moscow's guiding rule: Nothing that furthers the spread of Marxism-Leninism is immoral. To them, the evidence (which had grown to include gasmasks with high levels of mycotoxin residue and reports on rockets containing phosgene and hydrogen cyanide) told them but one story, and one by one they have sought to acquire their own C/B capabilities.

The Iran–Iraq War provides an excellent example of the difficulties involved in understanding and communicating what is happening in the world today. Iraq first began using chemicals, predominantly mustard, in 1983. In response, Iran published color brochures describing the attacks and presenting pictures of casualties in Iranian hospitals. However, this drew little international attention. Iran's credibility was so negligible that many observers viewed the Iranian claims as specious and manufactured.

In early March 1984, Iran mounted its "final offensive." The Iranians seized portions of Majnoon Island, which is believed to be sitting on yet another vast subterranean deposit of oil. Iraq counterattacked, but was turned back. Ultimately Iraq decided to use a combination of mustard and powerful nerve agents in an all-out effort to break the Iranian defense.

The attack was clear and unequivocal. No longer could the presence of chemical warfare be shrugged off as poor intelligence or inaccurate data collection. In an effort to gain publicity and marshal public support for their side of the conflict, Iran shipped casualties to several European hospitals for treatment, but the publicity was short-lived. Just as in Afghanistan and Southeast Asia, the casualties were regarded with skepticism and, in some quarters, downright hostility. Iran countered by inviting in an impartial UN team to inspect the area. The team arrived and within six days had uncovered incontrovertible evidence: an unexploded bomb filled with mustard and samples of soil containing Tabun, the first of the World War II German nerve agents. The skeptics were uncharacteristically silent.

In the months that followed, little attention was directed to the conflict, and to the effectiveness of the chemical agents. Rather, the news focused on efforts undertaken to stop the flow of chemicals into the area; increased publicity was directed to the "progress" made in the arms control negotiations in Geneva. Numerous complaints were sent to Iraq, which politely told people to direct their attention to Iran, not Iraq.

The latest drive was launched on 25 February 1986. Codenamed "Dawn 9," the Iranian offensive struck the strategic Fao peninsula. Iraq countered with even more modern nerve agents and the casualties ran up to five thousand per day in one counterattack. Still, the information hardly made the newspapers. The news media, for a variety of reasons, seem unwilling to recognize the modern reemergence of CBW and the motivations that drive proliferation.

The motivations are the essence of simplicity. General Rudini, the Indonesian Army chief of staff, has said Indonesia needs a biochem industry, among other reasons, because it would provide them with the base for biochemical warfare. This is important "because other parties are already using poisonous gas." Likewise, Israel has acquired its own C/B offensive and defensive capability. Syria is reported to have its own capability. In the early 1980s, Ethiopia, another Soviet proxy, was reported to be using chemical agents in its battles with the Eritrean rebels and in border skirmishes with Somalia. Soviet proxy forces in Angola—both the *Movimento Popular de Liberação de Angola* (MPLA) and Cuban assistance forces—are reported to have used phosphorus-filled projectiles and bombs against Angolan UNITA forces and civilian villages since 1975. Reports that the British found stocks of nerve agent in the Falklands supported Chile's concern that Argentina had begun to acquire chemical weapons, which was the reason given for Chile's decision to do likewise.

Another development, closer to home, is Cuba's acquisition of a CBW capability. Reports authenticating this development have come from émigrés, defectors, and captured Cuban soldiers. Two C/B facilities have been identified in Cuba. One is at Kimonor, in the province of Matanzas, where there is a special army school staffed with Soviet instructors. A second is at Jardín de Orquilles, which is close to the town of Soroa. The Kimonor plant was reported to have been built by Soviet technicians in 1981. Cuban nationals are not permitted in this plant. It is understood to have been producing Yellow Rain in conjunction with other plants in Cuba. The output is shipped to Poland, East Germany, the Soviet Union, and Afghanistan.

As reported by Cuban defectors, the Jardín de Orquilles facility is engaged in experimental development of germ warfare products and toxins. The latter are described as the type that can be introduced into a city water supply system. Soviet instructors at the chemical warfare school of the Cuban Revolutionary Army have claimed that toxins strategically placed in the Mississippi "could contaminate a third of the United States." To lend credence to the concepts, water supplies in both Kampuchea and Afghanistan have been poisoned with toxins.

The C/B research and production facilities in Cuba have been constructed underground (this was also true of the chemical warfare production plants in Czechoslovakia). Further, they are considered important enough (or dangerous enough) to warrant their own air defense sites. Reports have surfaced, as yet unauthenticated, associating the facilities with a high incidence of cancer in the proximate region, as well as with the sudden emergence of insidious and unexplained illnesses among Cuban soldiers guarding the facilities.

Those taken ill were reportedly sent to the Soviet Union for medical treatment. Cuba has been implicated in the training of the PLO and SWAPO in chemical warfare methods and techniques. In late 1983, an officer from the Cuban Revolutionary Army announced the establishment of an advanced chemical warfare training facility in Cuba.

Another Soviet proxy, Nicaragua, has been advertising chemical warfare "defense" capabilities. It is yet unknown whether this is done in mockery or as a serious warning to those who would challenge the Sandinista's right to rule the country. Nonetheless, the equipment is there, and training is under way. It may not be too long before Central America becomes another chemical warfare battlefield or a manufacturing site for advanced C/B agents. This would carry on the Soviet tradition of using C/B agents as a means of maintaining control in Third World revolutionary wars and of discouraging U.S. counterrevolutionary activity.

Scenario Twelve: Addis Ababa, Ethiopia

The ride over the rutted and potholed road into Addis Ababa was a less-than-auspicious introduction to the capital of Ethiopia, one of the ten poorest nations on earth. Knots of tiny black children— with distended stomachs and running sores on their parchment-like skin—converged on the ancient Mercedes at each stoplight. They tried to hawk miserable handicrafts, or simply to beg enough to survive for another day. Some were naked; others were clad only in ragged T-shirts given to them by the government. Emblazoned on the front were pictures of Lieutenant Colonel Mengistu Haile Mariam, the nation's strongman and African version of the "maximum leader." On the back were revolutionary slogans or scenes depicting "great moments" of his reign. At one stoplight, a young boy urinated on the side of the car while his older brother held up individual cigarettes for sale.

Some of the traffic lights were operated as toll lights. As the car approached a dusty intersection near the heart of the city, a policeman standing on the corner near the control box froze the light on red and waited for the driver of the car to provide him with a gratuity, which he did, rolling down the window and tossing the policeman a few coins.

In the mid-1950s, John Gunther wrote that Addis Ababa "looks as if it had been dropped piecemeal from an aeroplane carrying rubbish," and it is clear to the contemporary visitor that it has gone downhill ever since. Ethiopia's dusty capital is a monument to urban chaos, filth, and decay. It is a sea of mud; corrugated iron huts surround a bizarre collection of glass and steel skyscrapers and public buildings. Some are modern; others sport friezes and columns, survivors of the reign of Haile Selassie, the playactor Emperor and erstwhile "Lion of Judah," who presided for more than a half century over a feudal wasteland of misery and corruption. Whole facades had crumbled from buildings—even relatively new ones—and the debris was simply swept into heaps and left by the roadside. There was no sewer system in most of the city, a fact immediately obvious to anyone riding in an open car. Open gutters ran along the edge of the road. Most of the city's inhabitants relied on rain barrels for their drinking water.

Every wide spot in the road seemed to be presided over by a statue of Mengistu. Huge posters with his portrait adorned walls, and billboards (showing him in a variety of Homeric poses or exhorting the masses) had been erected at strategic intersections. It was rumored that the cult of personality had gone so far that Mengistu had even considered putting his portrait on the nation's flag, just as it was already on the country's worthless currency.

As the Mercedes bounded its way through the teeming city and approached a large military complex, the driver flicked a toggle switch beneath the dashboard, spewing out anthrax organisms from a generator mounted inside the car. The agent, which was expelled through a dummy exhaust pipe, appeared as smoky diesel exhaust to anyone observing closely. But, in a city where virtually every car burned oil, the "smoky" exhaust was unlikely to elicit any special attention.

The driver of the car was a Somali, and by the time he turned south on the road to Hosseina, he had saturated almost a dozen square kilometers of the city with pulmonary anthrax organisms.

The attack was in response to the Ethiopian use of nerve gas against Somali forces fighting for the control of the Ogaden, in a resurgence of the long-simmering conflict between the two nations. More than a thousand Somali troops perished after the Ethiopians caught a column of Somalis in the open, unprotected, and hit them with the nerve agent in cropduster fashion with low-flying aircraft.

The use of the C/B agents represented a significant escalation in the severity of the warfare in the region. Only a generation earlier, tactical bombing meant pulling the pin on a pineapple grenade, placing the grenade in a peanut-butter jar, and dropping it out of the window of a Piper Cub. When the jar hit the ground and shattered, releasing the lever, the grenade detonated. Now both Ethiopia and Somalia—two nations that couldn't even feed themselves—had joined the ranks of nations possessing weapons of mass destruction.

Within hours of the covert attack, thousands of Ethiopians had developed the first flu-like signs of pulmonary anthrax poisoning: chills, nausea, shortness of breath, fever, and respiratory distress. By the end of the first day, more than six thousand people were dead. Hospitals were overflowing with casualties, and the rich were paying bribes of $25,000 and more for treatment and a hospital bed. The poor, by contrast, were simply being left to their fate. After five days, the number of fatalities had risen to more than eighty thousand: the number of deaths resulting from the dropping of the atomic bomb on Nagasaki. Bodies littered the streets of Addis Ababa, the putrefying flesh drawing hordes of flies, rats, and vultures. The Ethiopian government seemed as oblivious to the sufferings of its population as it had been during the drought and famine that wracked the country in the mid-1980s; now it was more interested in attracting international relief funds and scoring propaganda points. Everyone is susceptible to pulmonary anthrax poisoning, and the disease has over a 93-percent mortality rate in untreated cases. But modern antibiotics, such as tetracycline, have proven effective in treating the infection, if administered rapidly and continuously after exposure. But such antibiotics are expensive and were in short supply in Ethiopia. Moreover, anthrax spores can live for years—even decades—in the environment, and presented the Ethiopian government with a massive cleanup problem.

Within days of the attack, Ethiopia retaliated against Mogadishu, the Somali capital, dropping hundreds of canisters of a crude nerve agent—toxin mixtures—and then sending over their crop-dusters in a final fly-by salute, as the outside world looked on in horror.

The Technological Impetus

However many nations have operational CBW capabilities, the important fact is that proliferation is a growing problem. It is not limited to the large industrialized countries. Nearly every nation is capable, technically and operationally, of producing at least rudimentary chemical, and in most cases biological, weapons, Relatively unskilled troops can transport the toxic substances, load the material into weapons, and deliver them on target.

It is not enough to say the threat is a terrorist threat, or a Soviet threat. Without question, the Soviet Union has provided the main stimulus. But it is not the only impetus in the spreading drive to acquire C/B weapons. The technology that has become universally disseminated and readily available in recent years is equally responsible for the growing problem.

Years ago, the proliferation of nuclear weapons was considered perhaps the greatest threat to international stability. Fortunately, this threat has been controlled, to some degree, by international safeguards, the reluctance of nuclear nations to share weapons technology, and because most nations have begun to question the very efficacy and usability of these weapons. The obvious solution to C/B weapons proliferation would be to limit the flow of technology and materials (just as has been done in the nuclear arena). However, even the most cursory examination reveals how difficult, if not altogether impossible, this would be.

There are, nevertheless, a number of similarities between C/B and nuclear weapons. The rationale for atomic weapons is obvious. As explosive weapons, atomic weapons offer thousands of times more explosive power than conventional weapons. Consider, for example, the technology of the Hiroshima bomb. It weighed approximately five thousand pounds, and possessed an explosive energy equal to ten thousand tons of TNT—that is, twenty million pounds of explosive energy in a five-thousand-pound bomb. Thus, the first crude atomic weapon represented a four-thousand-fold increase in explosive power over conventional TNT.

C/B weapons are also widely regarded as weapons of great potential effectiveness, and have long been categorized along with nuclear weapons as "weapons of mass destruction." This is, as in the case of atomic weapons, the basic reason behind the interests in CBW. In the early 1960s, Soviet military analysts considered chemical weapons to be roughly equivalent to lower-yield nuclear weapons. Today, when the potentials of current technology are added in, the comparison changes markedly—in favor of CBW. The improvements of the latest hydrogen bomb over the atomic bomb are dwarfed in comparison to the increases in effectiveness that are available through biotechnology. There is no leveling off in the biotechnology field as there is now in the nuclear field. Where we stand today is only the beginning.

Substances a thousand times more potent than the nerve agents of the 1960s can now be manufactured quite easily. Indeed, this was even done by two enterprising individuals in Springfield, Massachusetts, who set up shop, quite successfully, to manufacture the highly potent toxin ricin. And if the genetic engineering techniques developed in the late 1970s are applied, substances that are a million times more toxic can be manufactured, many with only minimal difficulty. With only a modicum of equipment, a good biologist can even turn friendly organisms into manufacturing plants that produce chemicals or proteins that are easily a billion times more potent than nerve agents.

But even more important then increasing toxicity or lethality, C/B agents can be programmed to eliminate or greatly suppress undesirable side effects (something that cannot be achieved with modern nuclear weapons). Agents can be tailored to attack only very specific cell complexes or chemicals in the body. Do you want to kill people? Simple. Do you just want to make them sick—very sick? This is also deceptively simple. Or do you want to alter their well-being, mental attitude, or acuity? This is not as simple, but nevertheless is possible; selectively and effectiveness are improving each year.

In other words, for someone looking for the ultimate in effectiveness and versatility, the new and coming generations of C/B weapons look mighty attractive.

Nuclear weapons also looked attractive in the beginning. However, many problems have retarded proliferation. This is where the differences between chemical, biological, or biochem weapons and nuclear weapons are most dramatic. What have been problems in the nuclear area are advantages in the case of C/B weapons.

First, there is the problem of secrecy—that is, guarding the fundamental knowledge needed to make a nuclear bomb. Notwithstanding publication of the basic bomb theory and the disclosure of selected design features during the trial of Julius and Ethel Rosenberg, most nuclear weapons techniques have been kept secret, and the design of an effective weapon is not an easy task.

In contrast, there is little secrecy about the scientific advances in the life sciences. With the exception of ongoing research and proprietary commercial processes, scientific advances in the life sciences are generally disseminated very rapidly. The advances spread laterally to various nations and cultures, and vertically to the lowest educational levels. Highly specialized techniques that first were developed in research laboratories five years ago are now routinely taught in undergraduate college courses. Equipment can now be purchased to manufacture substances that were only discovered a few years earlier.

Today, the biological and chemical sciences are being popularized. The terms, concepts, and techniques are working their way into the mainstream of society. This not only applies to new "sexy" techniques, such as gene splicing, but even more importantly to the techniques for making and using the older chemical and biological agents. There is even a recorded instance of a fourteen-year-old child manufacturing the powerful drug methamphetamine. The latest equipment and techniques available in nations like Libya and Saudi Arabia as they are in the best U.S. universities; some researchers would say they are even more available in those countries.

Most disturbing of all, there exists an international effort to transfer new biochem technology as fast and as widely as possible. A UN project to accomplish exactly this has been in operation for several years. Its objective is to encourage and assist the spread of biotechnology and genetic engineering around the globe. And every industrialized nation has a national effort to develop new techniques and low-cost production capabilities. The technology is spreading faster than computers and microelectronics. Again, this is an indication of how effective the popularization of the new sciences has been

Secondly, nuclear weapons require special materials and manufacturing equipment that are expensive and difficult to obtain. There are reasonably effective controls on critical equipment and materials, especially fissionable material. The manufacture of nuclear weapons is difficult. Moreover, it requires special, precision machine tools and electronics, the sales of which are closely monitored.

None of these problems are serious impediments for a country that desires to acquire a C/B weapons capability. As already noted, the technology and equipment are readily available. Even more important, C/B weapons, unlike nuclear weapons, are cheap. To be sure, some of the equipment is priced in the ten- to one-hundred-thousand-dollar range—for example, elaborate new items such as DNA synthesizers. Manufacturing facilities do not come cheaply. But they are no more expensive than a brewery, or pharmaceutical or insecticide plants; the latter can be used to produce a wide variety of C/B agents. Biochem weapons are affordable for any nation, and even for many individuals and terrorist groups. The only problem is deciding which opportunity to pursue.

For a mere pittance, any nation can achieve superpower status in C/B weapons. And though the weapons truly are the "poor man's atomic bomb," one should not assume that such weapons are, in any sense, poor or inferior weapons, to be denigrated or discounted by adversaries—especially superpowers or fanatics.

With C/B weapons, even the smallest nation can join "the first team." A commercial aircraft or a high-speed pursuit boat armed with a C/B agent dispenser could pose a major threat to an entire

U.S. naval task force, such as the one involved in the 15 April 1986 raid on Libya. Needless to say, the U.S. Navy would object to such a scenario, maintaining that chemical weapons do not sink ships. Unfortunately, though this is strictly true, people are required to run the ships. With one exception, our navy's ships are not protected against C/B agents that might be released upwind of a task force and engulf the ships and their crews without warning.

In the case of nuclear weapons, efforts to stop nuclear proliferation, although slow to take form, have been moderately effective. Considerable money and effort have been applied to the problem. Still, in certain cases nations have felt compelled to resort to extreme preemptive actions to safeguard their security, as in the case of the Israeli attack on the Iraqi reactor in June 1981.

At the same time, people are beginning to appreciate that there may be major limitations associated with the use of nuclear weapons. A nuclear weapon is still a nuclear weapon: Even the smallest detonations are relatively large, equivalent to tens of tons of high explosives. The use of a nuclear weapon simply is not a low-profile operation. Nor can one be used covertly. Some observers even maintain that nuclear weapons simply are not usable. Others are far less sanguine on this point, but do realize that there are many risks associated with nearly any potential use, and those risks are sufficiently great so as to bring into question the wisdom of trying to develop a nuclear capability in the first place.

Such reasons have contributed to the fact that nuclear proliferation—once the initial drive by the major powers to acquire such weapons was concluded—has proceeded at a relatively slow pace. In the case of C/B weapons, these reasons are all reversed; rather than retarding proliferation, they actually expedite it.

Modern-day technology has made possible the acquisition of a wide spectrum of biochem weapons that are cheap and very effective. The technology is widely available and proliferating rapidly Controls over chemicals can influence the rate of proliferation to some degree. But such controls can hardly stop a determined country, any more than they could stop a determined terrorist from ultimately obtaining biochem weapons.

Scenario Thirteen: Tripoli, Libya

Frank Saba had never been to Tripoli before. In fact, despite his Arab ancestry, Libya was the first Arab country he had ever visited. The invitation had been very mysterious: the phone call from a Dr. Omar; the first-class, round-trip ticket that arrived in the mail; and the promise of $10,000 for three days of consulting. That was un-heard-of money for a college professor, even though he was chairman of the microbiology department at one of the large state universities in the western United States.

He had been met at the airport by Dr. Omar and several security men, and escorted directly to a black Mercedes without having to pass through customs. The air conditioning was turned up full blast, and there was a country–western tape playing on the tape-deck, which surprised Frank and struck him as somewhat incongruous in the desert setting.

Dr. Omar noticed an anthology of Tennessee Williams's plays sticking out of the pocket of Frank's carry-on bag. Frank had bought it at the airport before he left. It had been a whim; he hadn't read a play in twenty years, but had always admired A Streetcar Named Desire *since he had attended a performance of it at his high school in California. Even the amateur acting had not dampened his enthusiasm.*

"Tennessee Williams," groaned Dr. Omar. "A homosexual writing plays about drunks and perverts. Decadent literature. If you must keep it, do not leave it lying around."

Frank was surprised by Dr. Omar's reaction. But I suppose there are rednecks in every culture, he told himself, too interested in the scenery flashing by to dwell on Dr. Omar's narrow-mindedness.

The landscape was bathed in the white light characteristic of desert regions—the strong white light that bleaches the color out of everything. As they came into Tripoli, a cloud of fine white dust followed the car along the sun-baked streets. The city seemed to be one massive construction site. There was so much building going

on, Dr. Omar told him, that a person could make a fortune just by
sweeping th cement dust from the streets.

Dr. Omar pointed out the lavender-domed palace of the former
crown prince as they passed by. It was now used to house guests of
the revolutionary government, Dr. Omar explained. There was a
red-yellow-green tricolor with a large "R" in the center flying next
to the red, white, and black Libyan flag. No doubt the President of
Rwanda was visiting, probably with hat in hand, promising to curse
and despise Jews and Zionists and their allies if only the Libyans
would ante up a little money to show their appreciation.

They moved rapidly along the monotonous street, the white-
washed walls of the low buildings dissolving into a blur before
Frank's eyes. Dr. Omar's driver threaded the Mercedes through the
traffic alongside the old seawall and the once fashionable prome-
nade. Two decades earlier, it had been one of the most lovely vistas
in North Africa, a shimmering white city spread along a broad cres-
cent of sand next to the blue sea. Now a huge docking area covered
the seafront. There were acres and acres of concrete covered with
thousands of tons of containerized cargo. There were tractors,
trucks, military vehicles, heavy equipment, and cement—mountains
of cement. Dozens of ships were unloading still more cargo, and
others were lying offshore waiting their turn for a berth in the over-
crowded port. Frank could see that many of the ships had Cyrillic
markings.

The driver eased the Mercedes around a crowded traffic circle.
In the center of the circle, several scraggly palm trees reached up
toward the thick white light. Banners strung between the trees pro-
claimed, "Revolution is the Citadel of Revolutionaries," in English,
French, and Arabic.

When they arrived at the Beach Hotel, they left the Mercedes
double-parked in front and passed through a cluster of security men
sitting around a battered wooden table in the foyer. They looked
Frank over like a band of Roman youths gaping at a comely young
woman, not subtly but with indolent leers.

After Frank checked in, Dr. Omar suggested they go out on the
terrace and get something cold to drink. The terrace was empty so
they took seats near the railing overlooking the Mediterranean. Dr.

Omar ordered drinks from the disinterested waiter. Frank's eyes scanned the long jetty reaching out into the sea a short distance down the beach. Several young boys on the end of the jetty were tossing rocks out into the dark choppy water. Further down the coast, he could see the stark lines of the new fortress-like villas clustered near the water's edge, monuments to the affluence of this oil-rich wasteland. The villas were deep green, bright blue, and mauve, not the gentle pastel colors of those on the other side of the Mediterranean.

The waiter brought them each a tall glass containing a dark red liquid. It was a bitter-tasting local soft drink, and Frank pushed it away after one swallow. Besides, the rim of the glass tasted as though it had been wiped with a dirty dishrag. Frank would have given anything for a cold beer, which (like all alcoholic beverages) was forbidden by law.

"Now that I'm here, maybe you'll tell me what this is all about," Frank inquired, no longer able to stifle his curiosity.

"You will know soon enough," responded Dr. Omar.

"Hey, wait a minute," bristled Frank. "I've taken time out of a busy schedule and traveled six thousand miles. You owe me an explanation."

"Perhaps you are right."

Dr. Omar gazed out into the vastness of the Mediterranean for several moments as if mulling the matter over, then turned his attention back to Frank. "Actually we invited you here for a meeting," began Dr. Omar, choosing his words carefully.

"With whom?"

"In fact, we want to talk to you about your future," continued Dr. Omar, ignoring Frank's question. "You should find the meeting very stimulating."

"Meeting? You brought me all the way over here for a meeting? Why couldn't we have had it in the States?"

"That would not have been possible," answered Dr. Omar.

"But who is this meeting with?" demanded Frank, his voice rising and taking on a hard edge, frustrated at not being able to pin Dr. Omar down or to extract any direct answers from him.

"Brother Colonel," responded Dr. Omar, pushing his chair from *the table and standing up. "There'll be a car around for you tomor-row morning at ten. Be ready." He pulled a thick roll of bills from his pocket and peeled one off and threw it down on the table. "Ciao."*

Brother Colonel? It took several moments for the words to reg-ister. Qaddafi! They've brought me over here to meet Qaddafi, Frank suddenly realized. The thought staggered him. What possible interest could the controversial (and some said not altogether sane) leader of the North African nation have in a microbiologist born in Sacramento, son of an immigrant Syrian greengrocer and his Le-banese wife? Frank opened his mouth to call after Dr. Omar, but his mysterious host had already disappeared.

Frank lingered for some time on the terrace, the salty breeze off the ocean cooling his face, trying to anticipate the nature of his meeting the following day. But as jet lag finally caught up with him and he wandered up to his room to get some rest, he was no nearer to figuring things out than before he had arrived.

It rained during the night as it often did in April. The streets still glistened with water when the car came to pick up Frank the following morning. Only a pale, sickly light seeped through the gray canopy of sky overhead.

"Where are we going?" Frank asked once they were underway.

"Ra's al-Hilal," Dr. Omar replied. "There's a plane standing by."

"What's Ra's al-Hilal?"

"You'll see when we get there."

At what used to be Wheelus Air Force Base on the eastern edge of the city, abutting the Mediterranean, they climbed aboard a sleek private jet for the five-hundred mile flight across the Gulf of Sidra to an airfield at Shahhat. At Shahhat, they were met by a Land Rover and transported a short distance to the coast, where they transferred to a high-powered speedboat manned by two black-garbed Eastern Europeans with MP5K submachine guns slung at their sides. The speedboat, its bow high in the air, skimmed over the water. They traveled east, hugging the coastline. By contrast to the gentle topography around Tripoli, the coastline here was a solid wall of gray cliffs rising several hundred feet or more vertically from the water's edge.

After a twenty-minute ride, as they approached a cleft in the rocky cliffs, the driver of the boat cut the engines and the bow settled down in the water. One of the men flashed a signal to the coastline and it was acknowledged by another flash from what appeared to be an observation post near the top of the cliffs. Then, its engines idling slowly, the speedboat eased cautiously toward the shadowy indentation in the jutting cliffs, which appeared to grow larger and larger before their eyes. Only then did Frank realize that it was a huge door, perhaps seventy feet high, carved out of solid rock.

The door rumbled open and they passed into a brightly lit cavern the size of a football field, ringed with metal scaffolding and catwalks.

"Welcome to Ra's al-Hilal," said Dr. Omar.

"Amazing."

"It was a German U-boat pen during World War II."

They docked at a small platform at the far end of the cavern and were escorted up several flights of stairs and through a tunnel into another large chamber full of activity. Men of many races and nationalities, wearing sand-colored chammies, were being drilled by black-clothed instructors in the finer points of hand-to-hand combat and parrying knife attacks. Others were running an obstacle course, shimmying up and down ropes, hurtling barriers and crawling beneath ribbons of concertina wire.

"This whole cliff is honeycombed with tunnels," explained Dr. Omar, as they turned into another corridor. They passed classrooms, a fully equipped gymnasium, a medical clinic, what appeared to be a laboratory and machine shop, until finally coming to a set of heavy metal doors. One of their escorts, dressed like all the others in black turtleneck, baggy trousers with cargo pockets, and jump boots, reached for a phone hanging from the wall and identified them.

Once clearance had been received, both the escort and Dr. Omar placed their right hands on top of a glass screen next to the door that fed their handprints into a computer where they were compared to prints on file in the computer's memory bank. Then Frank was instructed to do the same. "That way your print will be on file," he was informed. A green light flashed on the wall and the *four-inch-thick metal door rolled back, and they stepped into what was apparently an elevator. The escort punched a digital code on the control panel and the elevator ascended for several seconds. It jolted to a stop and a door at the rear of the elevator opened. Frank turned to find himself peering into a lavishly appointed room. The floor was covered with oriental rugs atop which sat low-slung Middle Eastern furniture smothered in plush pillows, many of them with elaborate designs. A thin gauzy material was suspended from the ceiling, lending a canopy effect to the scene and creating the illusion of being in a tent somewhere in the desert. There was a hint of incense in the air.*

It was like stepping into a scene from A Thousand and One Nights, *Frank told himself. It would have been an unusual setting anywhere, he reflected, but occurring as it did deep in the bowels of an old U-boat facility carved out of solid rock in Libya, it bordered on the fantastic.*

It took Frank several moments to adjust to the dim light inside the room. Gradually, a figure materialized at the far end of the room, seated cross-legged on a dark mat in front of a low table. Behind him were what appeared to be a half-dozen bodyguards, all of them women, and all of them attractive. They were clad in tight breeches and tunics, high-heeled boots, and military hats with short brims and flat crowns. They were standing motionless, at attention, submachine guns pressed tightly across their ample bosoms.

The figure on the mat was dressed in a spotless long white robe and there was a dagger stuck in his belt. He motioned Frank to come closer. Suddenly Frank was face-to-face with Libya's Brother Colonel, Muammar Qaddafi. There could be no mistaking the almost grotesquely large head, the bushy Afro, the lantern jaw. He looked almost like a caricature, Frank thought, with the enormous head perched atop the slight body.

Qaddafi indicated with a sweep of his hand for Frank to be seated at his side, then he clapped his hands together twice and a servant appeared with a tray on which were two cups and a pot of sweet tea.

"You'll take some tea, Dr. Saba?" asked the Libyan strongman in heavily accented English, each syllable carefully enunciated. Without waiting for an answer, he began to pour the steaming liq-

uid into the cups. It was only then that Frank realized that Dr. Omar and the escort officers had disappeared.

"Thank you for coming," Qaddafi told Frank in hushed tones. "I hope they have made you comfortable and attended to your needs."

"Quite comfortable."

"Good."

There was something fragile, almost feminine, about Qaddafi, Frank reflected. His hands were not strong hands, but rather artistic hands with long, thin fingers and neatly manicured nails.

"You are, of course, wondering why I summoned you here?"

Frank was still so overcome with the bizarre nature of his surroundings that he failed to pick up on Qaddafi's use of the word "summoned."

"Our revolution here in Libya must survive," continued Qaddafi, "for it is an instrument of Allah the Merciful and a beacon to the world. But it is beset by many enemies." *His eyes burned in his dark face as he spoke.* "And that is why you and your work are so important."

"My work?"

"Yes." *He picked up a folder off the table and waved it in front of Frank.* "You are an impressive man, Dr. Saba. A chemist, microbiologist, author of books and scholarly papers, a recognized expert on certain infectious diseases. And, most important of all"—*he paused and turned toward Frank, their two faces only inches apart*—"you are an Arab. A brother. The same blood runs through our veins."

"As an American, I am very proud of my Arab heritage," *responded Frank uncomfortably.*

"So as one Arab to another," Qaddafi said, *touching Frank lightly on the wrist,* "I want you to place your formidable skills in the service of your people . . . and of Allah." *He lifted his eyes heavenward.*

"That's very kind of you, but—"

"And we will pay you one million dollars a year and provide you with a house fit for a king, not to mention a luxury car and servants and whatever else pleases you."

A million dollars a year! Frank's heart skipped a beat. He wanted to quip: "Who do I have to kill?" but he remained silent. Qaddafi appeared to be a man who lacked a sense of humor.

"Did you say a million dollars a year?"

To a poorly paid college professor with two children about to attend university, a broken-down station wagon, and a long-suffering wife who made do without an electric dishwasher or the smart clothes and vacations enjoyed by many of their friends, it was nearly more than he could comprehend. He hadn't anticipated making a million dollars in his lifetime, let alone in one year.

"Indeed I did, my brother. And even more in the future perhaps. Libya is, after all, a land of endless horizons."

"And what could I possibly do . . . that would be worth such a munificent sum?" Frank knew there had to be a catch, he could feel it deep in his gut, but he was hooked and inwardly could feel his inhibitions slipping away. All he could see was the money, an end to the hand-to-mouth existence, the beginning of a new life free from the drudgery of teaching indifferent undergraduates and trying to churn out academic articles. He was ready to cry out, "I'll do it. Whatever it is, I'll do it. Just give me the money." Frank tried to appear cool and collected, as if he received such offers every day, even twice a day, but he knew he wasn't fooling anyone.

"We want to create a chemical and biological warfare capability," Qaddafi was saying. "An ultimate weapon to protect our revolution and ensure that the Zionists and Western imperialists cannot make us dance to their tune. A weapon we can share with brothers like Iran, who today suffers from Iraqi treachery in the form of chemical weapons that slaughter tens of thousands of true believers in the marshes of the Gulf. Our enemies have denied us nuclear weapons, but they cannot deny us these. The 'Moslem bomb' will be chemical or biological, not nuclear."

Frank was filled with a rush of emotions. He was always repulsed by the thought of chemical or biological warfare; it seemed to him the height of man's inhumanity to man. But now he was being offered a fortune to assist what was reputedly one of the most unpredictable and irresponsible governments in the world to develop such a capability. Did every man have a price, and had Qaddafi found his?

"Should you decline our most generous offer," Qaddafi said

very slowly, *"we will have little trouble, you must recognize, in finding someone else to take your place. Naturally, being one of us, you are our first choice and we hope you will not disappoint the brethren."*

"I-I don't know what to say," he stammered, more than just a little confused.

"You may now return to your university. In one week's time I will send a messenger for your decision. In the meantime, you are not to discuss this offer or any aspect of our meeting with anyone. I am certain you understand." Suddenly Qaddafi's composure changed from dead serious to relaxed and, smiling broadly and reaching out to seal the bargain with a limp handshake, he said with confidence, *"I look forward to your joining our cause. Your parents would be proud of you."*

Moments later, Qaddafi disappeared through a rear door, surrounded by his bodyguards. Frank was rejoined by Dr. Omar and one of the escort officers.

On the flight back to Tripoli, he sat alone, reflecting on the incredible past few days and the future. His instincts told him he was getting into something way over his head. Was this the proverbial pact with the Devil, or an opportunity to grab for the brass ring? He consoled himself with the thought that there is a fine line between madness and genius, and that men of great gifts sometimes cross back and forth over that line. Qaddafi was clearly an unusual man, but was he crazy? It was hard to tell. But, on the other hand, maybe it was all propaganda. Still further, he wondered, what would happen if he declined?

6
America the Vulnerable: Time for Action

> The backward look behind the assurance
> Of recorded history, the backward half-look
> Over the shoulder, towards the primitive terror.
>
> . . . .
>
> Not fare well,
> But fare forward, voyagers.
>
> T.S. ELIOT
> *Four Quartets*
> "The Dry Salvages," II, III

T ime is running out. America may one day come down with a cold produced in a Soviet, or even a terrorist, laboratory and never recover. We have entered a world far more dangerous than anyone imagined even a decade ago. It is a world where terrorists brew botulinus toxin in Paris bathtubs; where desperate Third World despots savage other nations with chemical weapons; where this country's enemies traffic in drugs and narcotics to undermine our society and make us pay for the cost of terrorist subversion around the world.

It is a world, moreover, where the Soviet Union has dedicated billions of rubles and the energies of literally thousands of its most brilliant scientists to perfecting terrifying new C/B agents against which the United States and the rest of the free world will be defenseless.

If we, as a nation, are not careful, we may end up as part of the silt of human history. Our passing will be grim testimony to the folly of inaction in the face of overwhelming danger, and of permitting those with what Baudelaire called "a thirst for extinction" to dominate our national life and our defense planning. Action does not always produce security, but we may be certain that inaction is a sure formula for disaster.

The United States faces two realities in this modern threat of C/B warfare. The first is the devastating potential of the new threat and the various forms it can take. The second is how ill-prepared the United States is at present to cope with the threat, even in its most rudimentary form.

The simple truth is that the United States has neither acknowledged the threat nor taken even basic steps to address it. None of the U.S. antiterrorist preparations are prepared to cope with a major C/B terrorist event. The drug and narcotics war is expanding, almost impervious to the attempts to contain it. The U.S. military is almost totally unprepared for sophisticated biochem sabotage. White House security is unable to detect, let alone respond to, many sophisticated threats. Should there ever be a general war in Europe, C/B weapons will play a significant role, and U.S. military plans to cope with this threat are ten to twenty years out of date.

This frightening state of affairs is attributable, in large measure, to bureaucratic indifference within the defense and national security establishments. There is a kind of crisis-input-overload mentality that desperately refuses to recognize the dramatic evidence now being accumulated on biochem threats. Among supposedly well-informed individuals, the severity of the threat is conceded, but they are overcome by a sense of hopelessness and a conviction that there are few, if any, effective steps that can be taken.

The United States, however, is not helpless. If we act responsibly and quickly, there are many measures that can be adopted to lessen the dangers posed by the chemical, biological, and even the high-tech biochem threat. Such measures will not win easy acceptance. They will require a substantial departure from past practices and a good deal of new thinking. In particular, there is an urgent need for U.S. policymakers to develop an appreciation of the seriousness of the threat and the need for an integrated and comprehensive response.

We believe the following set of actions is worthy of attention at the highest levels, not only in the United States, but in all concerned countries around the globe. Our main concern is the United States, but it is equally obvious that other nations are also at risk and that their supportive actions are essential in this most deadly and threatening war.

Biochem Advisory Council

Because of the impetus of biochemical science and technology as it relates to the problems of C/B warfare, it is imperative that an ongoing presidential advisory council be formed to review scientific developments and relevant intelligence and oversee U.S. CBW programs and preparations. The council would provide the president and cabinet with informed guidance and judgments relating to the CBW threat from adversaries, and the appropriate U.S. countermeasures. Composed of fifteen to twenty leading scientists and five to ten intelligence and operations specialists, the council would meet on a regular basis, and would be operationalized on a full-time basis in a crisis.

Intelligence

C/B matters are simply not subjects that the intelligence community addresses with the necessary diligence and understanding. Our perception of the problem is influenced by the fear and doubts that such weapons induce. It is difficult to get a clear picture of a subject so wrapped in unnecessary secrecy and confusion. It is no wonder, then, that our understanding should be fragmentary and incomplete.

A crash program is required to collect relevant data and to develop a comprehensive estimate of the present and future threats. Special attention must be paid to advanced technology, terrorism, and proliferation. Substantial improvement in intelligence analysis has been made since the early 1980s. But the effort is still inadequate. Even if the total effort devoted to biological and chemical intelligence were increased by a factor of ten, it would still be very small in comparison to the efforts directed to understand the nuclear threat.

Collection and analysis of data on the drug and narcotics trafficking operations—including the roles played by the Soviet Union and the People's Republic of China—should be a high-priority activity. The interface between these operations, terrorism of all varieties, including revolutionary war activity, and blackmail influence operations should be included in this investigation. In keeping with the dictum laid down by le Carré, this intelligence collection and analysis also should "follow the money."

It goes without saying that postattack countermeasures are a poor substitute for effective prophylactic efforts. It is equally clear that preemptive actions may be necessary when hostile powers choose to develop agents of a sufficiently deadly nature, or are tied to illegal drug and narcotics trafficking. To this end, intelligence associated C/B threats, including drugs and narcotics trafficking, should include a covert penetration and collection program that is significantly broader in scope and quality than existing efforts. Major steps should be taken to increase the effectiveness of U.S. intelligence penetration capabilities in all countries suspected of pursuing or hosting such activities.

The drug and narcotics operations being run against the United States are, arguably, a more present threat to the United States and other countries of the world than the nuclear threat. This should be reflected in the allocation of intelligence assets and efforts.

Internal Security

On the domestic front, just as internationally, good intelligence is the first line of defense against terrorism. Authorities have apprehended terrorists in several countries as they prepared to shoot down civilian jetliners with heat-seeking missiles. In each instance, they knew in advance of the terrorists' plans.

The imposition, however, of major restraints on the FBI and CIA during the mid-1970s has made it far more difficult for U.S. authorities to monitor violence-prone individuals and groups operating within the United States and to anticipate potential attacks. A major overhaul of the Levi–Smith guidelines may be the most important first step in restoring this nation's vital intelligence capability. The current guidelines prohibit the FBI from investigating individuals or organizations unless they are known to have committed or are about to commit a crime. Of equivalent importance is an amendment to the federal tort claims act that will provide protection to FBI investigators. Coordinated changes in the Freedom of Information and Privacy Acts are also essential.

Local police and law-enforcement officials should be given training to help them recognize the warning signs associated with the clandestine production of a C/B weapon, including the theft of certain kinds of laboratory equipment, break-ins at facilities where class-three pathogens are kept, and the disposal of animal carcasses used in testing. Most police departments and other state and county law-enforcement organizations would probably not make the connection between the discovery of specialized agent production gear or aerosol testing chambers and the likelihood that someone was attempting to build a C/B weapon.

The lack of effective controls on obtaining deadly specimen cultures or dangerous chemicals is a serious and potentially disastrous problem requiring urgent federal action. Similarly, the absence of uniformly rigorous standards governing the handling, storage, securing, and distribution of pathogens by universities and research institutes should be evaluated. The goal should be to make it more difficult for unauthorized persons to gain access to such facilities and the deadly cultures grown there, without impairing legitimate scientific research.

CBW Crisis Response Team

Numerous safeguards can be adopted, but there are no real defensive measures that are adequate to cope with the threat. The most important step that can be taken in advance of a crisis is the creation of an in-place response capability designed to react quickly and effectively at the first sign of trouble, perhaps patterned along the lines of the Nuclear Emergency Search Team (NEST).

Formed in 1974, NEST was created to deal with special nuclear incidents, including terrorist incidents involving fissionable or radioactive material. The organization, administratively attached to the Energy Department and operationally under the FBI, is a group of two to three hundred experts and consultants who are organized and prepared to respond on a moment's notice when a nuclear incident arises.

The government should form a counterpart organization whose mission would be to respond to C/B terrorism, acts of vengeance, and direct attack by a foreign power. The Biochem Advisory Council recommended above might well provide overall direction for the development and administration of such a team. The team will need to have techniques, equipment, support, data, liaison channels, and an organizational structure that are all a great deal different from those of NEST, insofar as the C/B problem is very different from the nuclear problem.

The CBW Crisis Response Team logically should be controlled by the FBI. The team likely will need to be created as a dedicated nongovernmental organization to enable the recruitment of appropriate experts and to foster the development of the necessarily close working relations with academic specialists, industrial laboratories, and all intelligence agencies. Major roles would be played by the Centers for Disease Control and the National Institutes of Health. The team might require extraordinary powers to respond to national crises—crises that could become emergencies of the highest magnitude.

Though the nuclear problem is potentially serious, most professionals have come to believe that C/B weapons pose a more serious threat, and one for which the United States has no counterpart capability. Certainly, there is no question that a unit with resources and funding at least equivalent to NEST should be created.

Covert Strike Force

Given the serious consequences of a C/B attack on the United States, and the extraordinary stakes involved in terms of potential casualties and disruption, no U.S. administration should simply sit back and wait for an attack to occur. If prior credible intelligence information is received suggesting that such an attack is imminent (or even a distinct possibility), forceful actions should be taken to eliminate or otherwise reduce the potential threat.

If the location and nature of the threat are known, the only prudent response is to preempt the attack, even if it involves striking another nation's territory. A good example of such a preemptive effort was the Israeli raid on the Iraqi nuclear reactor.

Where terrorists are involved, the terrorists' international patrons should be held responsible for any actions carried out by their surrogates. They should be retaliated against with strong economic and trade sanctions, and if those fail, military actions. Although such drastic measures rattle the faint of heart, the prevention of C/B attacks on the United States—perhaps the most bone-chilling threat faced by this country—is serious business and cannot be met with halfway measures or restraint.

Similar tactics are also warranted to combat drug and narcotics trafficking. As explained by Dr. Joseph Troiani, "Relying on treatment for the solution is like parking an ambulance at the bottom of a cliff. The only real way to do anything about the drug problem is to turn the problem off at the source."

Drug and narcotics trafficking amounts, in effect, to war by other, nonviolent means. In many respects it is more serious, more costly, and more disruptive of society than terrorism. The same techniques appropriate in combating terrorism should be applied to the drug problem, including direct action against those responsible, be they individuals or nations. Covert or regular military strike forces—whichever is appropriate—should be used to fight this trafficking. The French, for example, maintain a unit known as the Eleventh Shock Regiment, which is under the control of their intelligence community, and used only for retaliation (often covert retaliation). Perhaps the United States should consider the establishment of a similar unit, to be employed in grey-area wars, such as against terrorists, drug traffickers, their operating bases and (doubtful) sanctuaries. Where ships are involved in drug trafficking, those ships, independent of nationality, should be sunk. Where production takes place, those facilities and the people manning them should be destroyed. The residences of the drug kingpins and chieftains in Colombia, Mexico, Cuba, or any place else, should be targeted in the same way Colonel Qaddafi's residence in Libya was, although perhaps more discretely and without the accompanying fanfare.

Military Defense

Current defense programs are mainly structured to counter existing or probable threats of Soviet C/B agents. Because such intelligence is so limited and so old, major new emphasis must be placed on obtaining better intelligence. We must discover which agents the Soviets have (or are working on) so that U.S. policymakers can begin tailoring defensive measures to counter what might be described as a more realistic Soviet threat.

Nevertheless, such data will never be as accurate or complete as desired. Thus, an even more basic need is for a new approach designed to cope with both tactical and strategic surprise associated with the appearance of new agents. It took too long to learn what agents were being used in Southeast Asia and Afghanistan by the Soviets in 1975–84. Several years' time was unacceptably long; efforts were poorly organized, and did not include and countermeasure development activity. The defense and intelligence communities are only slightly better prepared today than they were in 1975. The intelligence and defense development communities need to have the capability to respond quickly when unknown agents are used. They must be able to determine what is being used, and must develop appropriate defenses and countermeasures, rather than just leisurely respond to requirements negotiated with the doctrine and material development bureaucracies.

The intelligence community and C/B R&D need to be restructured to respond to technology surprise. The problem is not just obtaining data in advance so that proper precautions can be taken, but rather preparing the system to react quickly and effectively to surprise when it occurs.

Additionally, a major revitalization of the C/B defense R&D community is called for. The army is the lead service in the defense establishment for chemical defense and has attempted to improve R&D over the past five years, but their programs remain dominated by traditional concepts and doctrine. This characteristic is not limited to the army technical laboratories. It is found throughout the defense community and reflects the distaste with which CBW is viewed. Direction for this to change has to come from the top.

Arms Control

In light of well-documented Soviet violations of both the 1925 Geneva Protocol and 1972 Biological and Toxin Weapons Convention, and evidence of their continuous and unabated expansion in CBW research, development, acquisition, and use since the early 1960s, there is only one honorable and sensible course of action for the United States. The United States should immediately withdraw from both those treaties (which have become only a sham), stating as its reason the record of Soviet violations. To remain a party to the treaties is to be an active participant in the charade and in so doing, give respectability to the Soviet actions.

Many political commentators assert that the best deterrent to the use of C/B weapons is a similar capability in the hands of the other side. Chemical weapons, they say, have only been used against an unprepared opponent. In World War II, the Germans did not use them because they were worried about the British and U.S. capabilities, and vice versa. Notwithstanding the billions of dollars the U.S. Army has spent on defense equipment for its forces in Europe, they are most adamant in stating their need for offensive deterrent munitions—defenses alone do not suffice.

Possession of C/B capability can also be an effective deterrent to conventional attack, as Iran has learned. No matter how many human sacrifices the aggressor is willing to offer up, C/B weapons can contain and defeat an attack. The message such a capability sends out is unmistakable: Watch out, because we are serious about our sovereignty.

Moreover, any nation that places any faith in arms control agreement or treaties in light of the events of the past decade deserves the consequences. As the old Russian proverb goes, "Even a fool is to be roughed up in church." The nations of the world can understand the events set in motion by the Soviets in 1963. The Soviets will use C/B weapons whenever an advantage is to be gained. They will be used to attack countries; to exterminate or drive out those who object to the Soviet form of government, imposed from the outside; they will be provided to Soviet proxies to be used as and when the occasion arises; and the various revolutionary and expeditionary forces under Soviet direction have been and will continue to be trained and equipped to fight with C/B weapons. This can only be regarded as a fact of life.

The acceptance of this perspective—distasteful as it might be to the pacifists and academics who earn their living championing arms control—has spread rapidly. There is no stopping it. We have entered a new age where the expanding presence of C/B weapons is a fact of life.

The question no longer is, Can proliferation be stopped? The question is, How do we understand who is doing what to whom, and what defenses or alternative responses can best help preserve the desired order?

Deterrence and Retaliation

Deterrence and retaliation are overworked words that are now used more to justify the absence of preparation to fight than the ability to fight. This distortion developed when the accountants, systems analysts, and new political strategists were given control of the Pentagon in the 1960s. Their mission was to "put the nuclear genie back in the bottle." War fighting was declared impossible and deterrence was equated with the "mere presence" of weapons, rather than a nation's capability to employ those weapons. This attitude matured during successive administrations as the Soviet military threat intensified—which the new leadership philosophy had decreed would not happen—while the U.S. "deterrent" fell victim to arms control imperatives and growing disinterest in countering the Soviet threat.

One need only review the chemical modernization program to understand the extent of what has happened. Since 1980, the Pentagon has been lobbying for binary shells and bombs that represent 1960s technology to "deter" the 1990 Soviet threat. And notwithstanding the numerous protestations on the obsolete nature of the current stockpile and the need for safer munitions, the binaries—complex and technically controversial—are to be built without ever having been tested in live firings. The latest development in 1986 is that the munitions are to be stored in the United States and then airlifted to Europe when the war is imminent, despite the fact that

Soviet military strategy calls for a lightning war where sabotage, surprise, special operations, and preemptive strikes are emphasized. the binary program is an excellent example of a program changing from the absurd to the ridiculous.

We need to give a great deal more thought and research to what types of weapons will be effective in stopping the Warsaw Pact forces. What is technically and operationally possible on both sides must enter into the consideration. Unfortunately, the offensive modernization program as it relates to CBW is neither the result of such deliberation nor of technical or operational requirements. Rather, it is driven by what has been on the R&D drafting tables for over twenty years. As privately stated by one of the leading official proponents of the modernization program, "I know it doesn't make much sense, but it's all we have."

Moreover, the critical issue is not binaries and the European theater. Rather, it is the United States. What is the biochem threat? What role might new agents play in Soviet plans for war? Should the United States reenter the race of effective biochem weapons? In pondering such questions, it is clear that new concepts of deterrence and retaliation—concepts that have *military* meaning—are required. It is inappropriate to speak of deterring attacks when there are no means for determining when the attack has begun or who is attacking.

Only the politically naive would suggest the United States respond to a C/B attack with nuclear weapons. Others would argue for a response in kind—but what does this mean? Should the United States respond in kind and begin trafficking in drugs and narcotics, or drug Soviet and Eastern European diplomats? Should a portion of the U.S. submarine-launched ballistic missile (SLBM) force be loaded with super biological warheads?

At present, at the very least, intense modern offensive biochem R&D programs should be initiated. There is no way short of such a program to understand how serious the offensive Soviet threat may be, or to understand the potential effectiveness of defensive measures. In the absence of the knowledge gained through such an effort, it is hard to understand how any informed decisions can be made whether the United States should reconstitute an effective biochem capability or what that capability should comprise.

The Internal Drug and Narcotics Problem

The drugs and narcotics problem is riddled with inconsistencies and misdirection. It is a simple truth that what will work cannot be known in advance. Equally true is what has and is being done has not worked. New approaches are needed.

The vast majority of studies of illegal drug and narcotics deal with unworkable laws that only serve to drive up prices and make trafficking a profitable venture. Certainly, one approach might be to cause the prices to drop to such an extent that the illegal operation is no longer profitable. Though the action required in this approach (which is to legalize sales) is hard for many to contemplate, the action may seem less radical when the effect of designer drugs on existing laws is recognized.

Certainly, consistency is required. All drugs should receive equal treatment, whether we refer to cigarettes, alcohol, marijuana, heroin, amphetamines, LSD, or fentanyl analogues. For those who want to use them, they should be available at a price so low as to drive the illegal trafficking out of business. Tax them, but no so high as to make trafficking profitable. Needless to say, this should also eliminate impure products and those drugs with permanently disabling impurities.

The undesirable-use aspect should be attacked through effective education and related advertising, similar to the antismoking campaign that was carried out in the early 1970s. Antidrug advertising (anti–all drugs) should be prominently featured on television and in reading material. For every product advertised, the advertiser might be required to cover the cost of two advertisements against the product. This campaign should be also carried into the schools, where children should be educated about the problems and health risks caused by drugs—all of them.

Illegal trafficking of all forms should be made a capital felony for all but the user. The user should be regarded as the victim, not the criminal. And, the laws should cover all dimensions of the trafficking problem and be enforced. The laws should extend to the financial apparatus that is involved—the large banks, independent of their location. If a bank is involved, its officers and directors should be prosecuted under the law as common felons.

Technology Transfer

Unlike the monitoring and control of nuclear technology, fissionable material, and the equipment needed to manufacture a bomb, no such parallel procedures exist with respect to C/B weapons technology and materials. Some equipment can and should be monitored. The advice of the Biochem Advisory Council should be used to determine where the guidelines should lie. This applies to data—such as is now freely available via computer terminals—as well as equipment. It would also apply to chemicals, cultures, cell fragments, techniques, and procedures.

However, attempts to control the spread of technology must not ignore that the biotechnological applications have such a great potential to improve the health and well-being of people everywhere. The transfer of technology should not be blocked, but often encouraged. Accordingly, discussion of the transfer problem will need to walk a fine line. The nature of this procedure may entail knowing how equipment and chemicals are to be used. Mechanisms should be tied to purchase agreements that will enable such transfers to be monitored to ensure that the equipment and chemicals are not being diverted to nefarious purposes. What the equipment is used for is difficult to hide. Similar checks on data-base access, a very critical aspect of technology transfer, might be devised.

Warnings of dangerous transactions would be facilitated if all applications for commercial transactions with communist countries and nations that are identified as state supporters of terrorism were made public. Let journalists and the public know who is selling what to whom. It is almost inconceivable, but even top National Security Council officials have found it difficult to pry such critical information out of the Commerce Department. As demonstrated in the nuclear proliferation arena, public exposure can stimulate considerable self-policing.

Selected List of
C/B Incidents by
Terrorists and
Other Nonstate Actors

1944, November	Plot by the Mufti of Jerusalem and German Nazis to poison the wells of Tel Aviv. The authorities discovered ten containers, each holding enough poison to kill 10,000 people.
1972, January	Two youths in Chicago arrested for plotting to introduce typhoid into the city's water system.
1972	Terrorist plot to use CW agents in an attack on a U.S. nuclear storage site in Europe uncovered.
1974, August	Muharem Kerbegovic, the so-called "Alphabet bomber," arrested in Los Angeles after mailing toxic material to a Justice of the U.S. Supreme Court and threatening to kill the President with a home-made nerve agent weapon.
1974, November	Forty-eight people, including the head of the Naples Port Agency, tried on charges arising from a 1973 cholera outbreak.

1976	A nerve agent (sarin) was brought into the United States by Michael Townley for use in an assassination plot against former Chilean Foreign Minister Orlando Letelier. The agent had originally been produced by Chile for possible use against Argentina or Peru, and was smuggled into the U.S. in a Chanel No. 5 atomizer.
	Subsequent reports surfaced that anti–Castro Cubans in the United States had learned of the Chilean-produced sarin and had asked DINA, the Chilean intelligence organization, for some in connection with their activities.
1976	One kilogram of a precursor of sarin was produced by a chemical engineer in Vienna and offered to bank robbers for 14,000 DM.
1978, February	The Arab Revolutionary Army Palestinian Commandos claimed responsibility for injecting a poisonous solution of mercury into Israeli citrus products.
1978	Libya sent a poison gas letter to a PLO official visiting Tripoli.
1978, September	Assassination of Bulgarian defector Georgi Markov in London using ricin umbrella weapon.
1978, October	Attempted assassination of Bulgarian defector Vladimir Kostov in Paris using ricin umbrella weapon.
1978–1979	Four hundred kilograms of intermediated compounds that could be used for organophosphorous nerve agents were discovered in a terrorist safe house in West Germany.

1979	A shipboard outbreak of gastroenteritis was determined to have been caused by a chemical agent.
1979	Attempted Soviet assassination of Afghanistan President Amin by a cook, who poisoned his food.
1980	Assassination of CIA agent Boris Korczak in McLean, Virginia (Tyson's Corner), using ricin weapon, possibly in umbrella configuration.
1980	Bathtub production of botulin toxin by German Red Army Faction discovered in a safe house at 41A Chaillot Street in Paris.
1980, August	Iraq cleaned out the Syrian Embassy in Baghdad and invited the Syrians to send in a new team of diplomats without the explosives, guns, and vat of poison discovered on the premises when it was raided.
1980	Several embassies in Europe received threats of terrorist use of a mustard agent against them.
1981, January	A Towson State University professor, convicted of shoplifting, attempted to kidnap the store manager in an act of revenge. After a struggle, the professor was arrested. In his car the police discovered a propane cylinder with a gear-driven motor (battery powered) to open the valve (controlled by a clock timer delay). The cylinder contained hydrogen cyanide gas.
1981, May	Herbicide contamination of food items in British grocery stores is discovered.

1981, October   Protestors claimed to have taken infected soil from the Herbidean island of Gruinard and placed it at the chemical defense establishment at Porton Down. The island has been closed to the public since germ warfare experiments on sheep were conducted there in 1941. The anthrax spores used in the experiments can remain dangerous for decades.

1983, March   The President of the Human Rights Commission of El Salvador was killed while investigating reports that the Army was using chemical weapons against civilians.

1983, May   The Israeli government reported that it had uncovered a plot by Israeli Arabs to poison the water in Galilee with an unidentified powder.

1983/4, Spring   The FBI obtained one ounce of ricin in a 35-mm film canister from an individual in Springfield, Massachusetts, who had manufactured it himself. This is believed to be one of several confiscations of ricin.

1984   A Cuban CW instructor defected and testified that Cuba has a stockpile of toxins. "If strategically placed in the Mississippi River," he contended, the toxins would be sufficient to "contaminate one-third of the U.S."

1984, January   A prisoner threatened to release the foot-and-mouth disease virus among livestock in Queensland, Australia, if prison reforms were not undertaken.

1984, September   Restaurants in Oregon were contaminated with *Salmonilla typhimurium*. Rajneesh subsequently implicated an aide.

1984	Tylenol contaminated with arsenic was found in drug and grocery stores. Several deaths resulted.
1984, November	Two Canadians attempt to procure tetanus and botulism cultures from ATCC. Reportedly the first phone order, of less deadly cultures, is filled, and it is not until the second order that ATCC employees become sufficiently suspicious to notify authorities.
1985	Coffee in an Israeli military mess was contaminated with the nerve agent carbamate.
1985	Soft drink and milk dispensers in Japan were dispensing cartons/bottles that had been contaminated by the addition of paraquate.
1986	More contaminated Tylenol was found in U.S. drugstores.

Note: In addition to the incidents included above, the authors are aware of several dozen others which cannot be released at this time. Moreover, many incidents are not recognized for what they are and therefore go unreported.

Selected References

Classic CBW

Defense Intelligence Agency, *Soviet Chemical Weapons Threat*, Washington, D.C., 1985.

Department of Defense, *Continuing Development of Chemical Warfare Capabilities in the USSR*, Washington, D.C., October 1983.

Department of Defense, *Soviet Military Power—1984*, Washington, D.C., March 1984.

Lois R. Ember, "Worldwide Spread of Chemical Arms Receiving Increased Attention," *Chemical and Engineering News*, 14 April 1986.

Siegfried Franke, *Manual of Military Chemistry*, Deutscher Militärverlag, East Berlin, 1967, JPRS CN-787-67.

Manfred Hamm, *Chemical Warfare: The Growing Threat to Europe*, Institute for European Defense and Strategic Studies, London, 1984.

Robert Harris and Jeremy Paxman, *A Higher Form of Killing*, Hill and Wang, New York, 1982.

Walter Hirsch, *Soviet Chemical Warfare and Biological Warfare Preparations and Capabilities—1935–1945*, translated by Zaven Nalbandian, Intelligence Branch, Office of the Chief, Chemical Corps, U.S. Army, 1951, declassified 6 June 1974 by Foreign Science and Technology Center.

Amoretta M. Hoeber, *The Chemistry of Defeat: Asymmetries in U.S. and Soviet Chemical Warfare Postures*, Institute for Foreign Policy Analysis, Inc., Cambridge, Mass., 1981.

Humans Used as Guinea Pigs in the Soviet Union, Hearings before the Subcommittee to Investigate the Administration of the Internal Security Laws Act and Other Internal Security Laws, Committee on the Judiciary, Senate, 30 March 1976.

N.I. Kaarakchiev, *Toxicology of Chemical Warfare Agents and Defense against Weapons of Mass Destruction*, Meditsina Tashkent, 1973, FSTC Translation FSTC-HT-0734-75.

General Frederick J. Kroesen (ret.) et al., *Chemical Warfare Study: Summary Report*, IDA Paper P-1820, Institute for Defense Analyses, Alexandria, Vir., February 1985.

Report of the Chemical Warfare Review Commission, Washington D.C., June 1985.

Brad Roberts, "Chemical Weapons: A Policy Overview," *Issues in Science and Technology*, Spring 1986.

William F. Scott, *Soviet Declaratory Views on Chemical and Biological Warfare*, Unpublished report prepared for Aerospace Medical Research Laboratory, U.S. Air Force, April 1984.

Edward M. Spiers, *Chemical Warfare*, University of Illinois Press, Urbana, 1986.

Hugh Stinger, *Deterring Chemical Warfare: U.S. Policy Options for the 1990s*, Foreign Policy Report Series, Institute for Foreign Policy Analysis, Inc., Cambridge, Mass., April 1986.

Textbook of Military Chemistry, Military Publisher of the German Democratic Republic (UEB) East Berlin, 1977, AD-B0629131L.

Nicholas Wade, "Biological Warfare: Suspicions of Soviet Activity," *Science*, 2 April 1976.

Mitchel L. Zoler, "Biochemical Assault: Is There Such a Thing as Preparedness?, *Medical World News*, 28 October 1986.

Soviet Psychiatric Abuse

Harvey Fireside, *Soviet Psychoprisons*, W. W. Norton and Company, New York, 1979.

Vladimir Golyakhovsky, *Russian Doctor*, trans. Michael Sylwester and Eugene Ostrovsky, St. Martin's/Marek, New York, 1984.

Alexander Podrabinek, *Punitive Medicine*, Karoma Publishers, Ann Arbor, 1980.

Eric Stover and Elena O. Nightingale, M.D., eds., *The Breaking of Bodies and Minds*, W. H. Freeman and Company, New York, 1985.

Modern Technology

ABC Weapons, Disarmament and the Responsibility of Scientists, Executive Council of Gewerkschaft Wissenschaft for the World Federation of Scientific Workers, London, 1972.

Rudy M. Baum, "New Variety of Street Drugs Poses Growing Problem," *Chemical and Engineering News,* 9 September 1985.

W. H. Breen, R. W. Gibson, S. B. Radding, G. F. Sirine, and A. G. Brown, *Microencapsulation,* SRI Technical Report no. 17, Stanford Research Institute, Menlo Park, California, June 1967, AD823785.

Commercial Biotechnology: An International Analysis, U.S. Congress, Office of Technology Assessment, OTA-BA-218, January 1984.

Joel Davis, *Endorphins: New Waves in Brain Chemistry,* Dial Press, New York, 1984.

Joseph D. Douglass, Jr., and H. Richard Lukens, "The Expanding Arena of Chemical–Biological Warfare," *Strategic Review,* Fall 1984.

Karl Drlica, *Understanding DNA and Gene Cloning,* Wiley, New York, 1984.

Douglass J. Feith, *Testimony on Biological and Toxin Weapons before the Subcommittee on Oversight and Evaluation of the House Permanent Select Committee on Intelligence,* Department of Defense, 8 August 1986.

Joseph Finder, "Biological Warfare, Genetic Engineering, and the Treaty That Failed," *Washington Quarterly,* Spring 1986.

Judith Hooper and Dick Teresi, *The Three-Pound Universe,* Macmillan Publishing Company, New York, 1986.

William Kucewicz, "Beyond Yellow Rain," *Wall Street Journal,* 23, 25, and 27 April, 1, 3, 8, 10, and 18 May, and 28 December 1984.

National Academy of Sciences, *Research with Recombinant DNA,* National Academy of Sciences, Washington, D.C., 1977.

Steve Prentis, *Biotechnology: A New Industrial Revolution,* George Braziller, Inc., New York, 1984.

Scientific American, Special Issue on the Molecules of Life, October 1985.

Soviet Military Concepts, Directorate of Soviet Affairs, Air Force Intelligence Service, No. 2-85, No. 3-85.

Edward J. Sylvester, and Lynn C. Klotz, *The Gene Age,* Charles Scribner's Sons, New York, 1983.

Anthony T. Tu, "Snake Neuro- and Necrotic Toxins: Potential New Agents," *NBC Defense and Technology International,* May 1986.

Jonathan B. Tucker, "Proteins to Order," *High Technology,* December 1985.

Jennifer Van Brunt, "Neuropeptides: The Brain's Special Messengers," *Bio/Technology,* February 1986.

James D. Watson et. al., *Recombinant DNA: A Short Course,* Scientific American Books, New York, 1983.

Raymond Zilinskas, "Biotechnology in the USSR," *Bio/Technology,* July 1980.

Terrorism

Shlomi Elad and Ariel Mera, *The Soviet Bloc and World Terrorism,* Paper no. 26, Jaffee Center for Strategic Studies, Tel Aviv University, distributed by Westview Press, Boulder, Colorado, August 1984.

International Terrorism, Insurgency, and Drug Trafficking: Present Trends in Terrorist Activity, Joint Hearings before the Committee on Foreign Relations and the Committee on the Judiciary, Senate, 13, 14, and 15 May 1985.

Harvey J. McGeorge II, "Bugs, Gas and Terrorists," *NBC Defense and Technology International,* May 1986.

Robert K. Mullen, *The Clandestine Use of Chemical or Biological Weapons,* Clandestine Tactics and Technology, International Association of Chiefs of Police, Gaithersburg, Md., 1978.

Neil C. Livingstone, *The War against Terrorism,* Lexington Books, Lexington, Mass., 1982.

Neil C. Livingstone and Terrell E. Arnold, *Fighting Back: Winning the War against Terrorism,* Lexington Books, Lexington, Mass., 1985.

Neil C. Livingstone and Joseph D. Douglass, Jr., *CBW: The Poor Man's Atomic Bomb,* Institute for Foreign Policy Analysis, Inc., National Security Paper no. 1, Cambridge, Mass., January 1984.

Uri Ra'anan et al., *Hydra of Carnage,* Lexington Books, Lexington, Mass., 1985.

The Role of Cuba in International Terrorism and Subversion, Hearings before the Subcommittee on Security and Terrorism, Committee on the Judiciary, Senate, 26, February, 4, 11, and 12 March 1982.

Edith Kermit Roosevelt, "'Germ War'," *International Combat Arms,* July 1986.

Terrorism: The Role of Moscow and Its Subcontractors, Hearing before the Subcommittee on Security and Terrorism, Committee on the Judiciary, Senate, 26 June 1981.

Terrorism and Other "Low-Intensity" Operations: International Linkages, Conference Report, Institute for Foreign Policy Analysis, Inc., Cambridge, Mass., 17–19 April 1985.

Drugs and Narcotics

Rudy M. Baum, "New Variety of Street Drugs Poses Growing Problem," *Chemical and Engineering News,* 9 September 1985.

Edward M. Brecher and the Editors of *Consumer Reports, Licit and Illicit Drugs,* Little, Brown and Company, Boston, 1972.

Bulgarian–Turkish Narcotics Connection: United States–Bulgarian Relations and International Drug Trafficking, Hearings and Markup before the Committee on Foreign Affairs and its Subcommittee on Europe and the Middle East, House, 7 June, 24 July, and 26 September 1984.

Castro's Narcotics Trade, The Cuban–American National Foundation, Inc., Washington, D.C., 1983.

Cocaine Abuse and the Federal Response, Hearing before the Select Committee on Narcotics Abuse and Control, House, 16 July 1985.

The Cuban Government's Involvement in Facilitating International Drug Traffic, Joint Hearing before the Subcommittee on Security and Terrorism, Committee on the Judiciary; the Subcommittee on Western Hemisphere Affairs, Foreign Relations Committee; and the Senate Drug Enforcement Caucus, Senate, 30 April 1983.

Designer Drugs, 1985, Hearing before the Subcommittee on Children, Family, Drugs, and Alcoholism, Committee on Labor and Human Resources, Senate, 25 July 1985.

Drug Abuse in the Military, Hearing before the Subcommittee on Children, Family, Drugs, and Alcoholism, Committee on Labor and Human Resources, Senate, 27 June 1985.

Drugs and Terrorism, 1984, Hearing before the Subcommittee on Alcoholism and Drug Abuse, Committee on Labor and Human Resources, Senate, 2 August 1984.

Gerd Hamburger, *The Peking Bomb,* Robert B. Luce, New York, 1975.

Impact of the South Florida Task Force on Drug Interdiction in the Gulf Coast Area, Hearing before the Subcommittee on Security and Terrorism, Committee on the Judiciary, Senate, 28 October 1983.

International Narcotics Control Report, Hearing before the Subcommittee on Children, Family, Drugs, and Alcoholism, Committee on Labor and Human Resources, Senate, 13 March 1985.

International Narcotics Policy, Hearing before the Select Committee on Narcotics Abuse and Control, House, 22 June 1983.

International Study Missions: Summary Report 1984, Select Committee on Narcotics Abuse and Control, House, May 1984.

Robert M. Julien, *A Primer of Drug Action,* 4th ed., Freeman, New York, 1985.

Narcotics Production and Transshipments in Belize and Central America, Hearing before the Committee on Foreign Affairs, House, 27 June 1985.

Recent Developments in Colombian Narcotics Control, Hearing before the Committee on Foreign Affairs, House, 24 May 1984.

Role of Nicaragua in Drug Trafficking, Hearing before the Subcommittee on Children, Family, Drugs, and Alcoholism, Committee on Labor and Human Resources, Senate, 19 April 1985.

Scope and Impact of Narcotic Trafficking in Alaska, Hearing before the Subcommittee On Children, Family, Drugs, and Alcoholism, Committee on Labor and Human Resources, Senate, 30 August 1985.

South Florida Local Law Enforcement Conference, Hearing before the Select Committee on Narcotics Abuse and Control, House, 14 May 1984.

Sports and Drug Abuse, Hearing before the Subcommittee on Alcoholism and Drug Abuse, Committee on Labor and Human Resources, Senate, 25 September 1984.

U.S. Narcotics Interdiction Programs in the Bahamas, Hearings before the Committee on Foreign Affairs, House, 28 September, 19 October, and 2 November 1983.

Communist Strategy

John Barron, *KGB: The Secret Work of Soviet Secret Agents,* Bantam Books, New York, 1974.

Richard Deacon, *The Chinese Secret Service,* Ballantine Books, New York, 1974.

John J. Dziak, "The Soviet Approach to Special Operations," in *Special Operations in US Strategy,* National Defense University Press in cooperation with National Strategy Information Center, Inc., US Government Printing Office, Washington, D.C., 1984.

Chapman Pincher, *The Secret Offensive,* Sidgwick and Jackson, London, 1985.

Jan Sejna, *We Will Bury You,* Sidgwick and Jackson, London, 1982.

Jan Sejna and Joseph D. Douglass, Jr., *Communist Decision Making: An Inside View,* Institute for Foreign Policy Analysis, Inc., Cambridge, Mass., 1985.

Soviet Covert Actions (The Forgery Offensive), Hearings before the Subcommittee on Oversight, Permanent Select Committee on Intelligence, House, 6 and 19 February 1980.

Andrei Y. Vyshinsky, *The Law of the Soviet State,* Macmillan Company, New York, 1948.

Arms Control and Proliferation

Peter Dunn, "The Chemical War," NBC *Defense and Technology*, April 1986.

Robert L. Bartley and William P. Kucewicz, "'Yellow Rain' and the Future of Arms Agreements," *Foreign Affairs*, Spring 1983.

The President's Unclassified Report to the Congress on Soviet Noncompliance with Arms Control Agreements, 1 February 1985.

Mark C. Storella, *Poisoning Arms Control: The Soviet Union and Chemical/Biological Weapons*, Institute for Foreign Policy Analysis, Cambridge, Mass., June 1984.

The Sverdlovsk Incident: Soviet Compliance with the Biological Weapons Convention, Hearing before the Subcommittee on Oversight, Permanent Select Committee on Intelligence, House, 1980.

W. Andrew Terrill, Jr., "Chemical Weapons in the Gulf War," *Strategic Review*, Spring 1986.

U.S. Department of State, *Chemical Warfare in Southeast Asia and Afghanistan, Special Report no. 98*, 22 March 1982.

U.S. Department of State, *Chemical Warfare in Southeast Asia and Afghanistan: An Update*, Special Report no. 104, November 1982.

U.S. Department of State, *Chemical Weapons: Arms Control and Deterrence*, Current Policy no. 409, 13 July 1982.

Index

About the Authors

Joseph D. Douglass, Jr., is a national security affairs consultant residing in McLean, Virginia. His specialties include Soviet political and military strategy, nuclear war, intelligence, and U.S. defense planning. Dr. Douglass is author or coauthor of ten books on U.S. and Soviet defense matters, including *Soviet Military Strategy in Europe, Soviet Strategy for Nuclear War,* and *Communist Decision Making: An Inside View,* and has lectured extensively throughout the United States.

Neil C. Livingstone is a Washington-based consultant on terrorism and national security matters. In addition, he presently serves as president of the Institute on Terrorism and Subnational Conflict, adjunct professor in the Georgetown University national security studies program, and consultant to ABC News "20/20." He is a frequent media guest and public speaker, and is the author of *The War against Terrorism* and *Fighting Back: Winning the War against Terrorism* (with Terrell E. Arnold).

Credits and Permissions

The authors wish to thank Harcourt Brace
Jovanovich, Inc., and Faber and Faber Limited
for permission to reprint the lines on p. 169
from "The Dry Salvages" in *Four Quartets*
by T.S. Eliot, copyright 1943 by T.S. Eliot,
renewed 1971 by Esme Valerie Eliot.

Credits for photographs, drawings, and cartoons following page 78:
American troops: AP/Wide World Photos
"Yellow Rain": S. Kelley
Chemical weapons victim: AP/Wide World Photos
Pandora's Box: Barling in the *Christian Science
      Monitor* © 1984 TCSPS
UN delegation: AP/Wide World Photos
Projectojet and Projectojet in use:
      Courtesy Harvey J. McGeorge
Drawings of attack on movie theater:
      Courtesy of Harvey J. McGeorge
"Hear no Soviet chemical warfare":
      © 1982, Washington Post Writers
"Produce Chemical Weapons?!": S. Kelley
Test grid: Courtesy of the Department of Defense
Scud B: Courtesy of the Department of Defense
Soviet troops: Courtesy of Harvey J. McGeorge
Weapons depots: Courtesy of the Department of Defense
"The administration claims": Tribune Media Services
Umbrella gun: *NBC Defense & Technology International*,
      vol. 1, no. 2 (May 1982), p. 60
Drawings of phony car exhaust, attack on airbase,
      and dumptruck: Courtesy of Harvey J. McGeorge
Send in the Clones: Courtesy of Larry Slot,
      Genemsco Corporation, 10 Braintree Ave., Kingston, MA 02364